The History of Paris

The History of Paris
from Caesar to Saint Louis

Maurice Druon

Translated from the French by
Humphrey Hare

Rupert Hart-Davis LONDON 1969

First published in French as
Paris de César à Saint Louis
by Librairie Hachette
© Maurice Druon and Librairie Hachette 1964
This translation © Rupert Hart-Davis
and Charles Scribner's Sons 1966

First published by Rupert Hart-Davis 1969
3 Upper James Street, Golden Square, London W1

Printed in Great Britain by
Ebenezer Baylis and Son Ltd
The Trinity Press
Worcester, and London

SBN 246 64308 0

To my Mother

Contents

List of Plates

Introduction

'Paris has had my heart from my childhood. I am French only through
this great city, great above all things and incomparable in its variety,
the glory of France and one of the most noble ornaments of the world.'

When Montaigne wrote those words, Paris had been in existence for
sixteen centuries and covered some twelve hundred acres. Today,
Paris covers more than twenty-four thousand acres. In four centuries,
the capital has multiplied itself twenty times.

Montaigne would recognise nothing of the Paris in which he once
lived except Notre-Dame, the spire of the Sainte-Chapelle, the Tour
Saint-Jacques, a fragment of the Louvre and a few walls of Cluny. In all
the rest, streets, houses, transport, commerce and sounds, he would
find nothing he knew except an occasional street-name. Perhaps only
the looks and bearing of the students would be familiar to him as they
daily emerge from the buildings of the Sorbonne and pass his marble
effigy, which sits unceremoniously, legs crossed, on the level of the
passer-by and of life. But the Rue des Écoles, where his statue has been
set up in recent times, with its handsome inscription on the plinth,
would be an unknown street to him.

Nevertheless, Paris is still the same city, since when we talk of it,
describe it or sing its praises we can still do so in Montaigne's words,
without changing a single one of them. The centuries wear away stones
quicker than they wear away words.

The greatness and permanence of a city lie in the deeds, sufferings,
tragedies and dreams of the successive generations of men who have
lived in it, and whose memory survives their habitations. In adding
one more to the many acts of homage paid to my native city I have

followed my inclination as a novelist. I have sought above all, amid the mists of its early history, to distinguish the figures of men, those whose deeds, linked together, have created its legend and woven its destiny.

MAURICE DRUON

Chapter 1

The Daughter of Rome

1 CAESAR'S CHOICE

THERE ARE PLACES which are born to be capitals of civilisation, just as there are men destined for the great tasks of history. Nothing appears to single them out until some sign from destiny points to their vocation and at the same time reveals them to the world.

Nothing distinguished the Island of Lutetia from a hundred similar islands, set like so many emeralds in the unfastened necklace of the Seine. Nothing had yet drawn attention to this Gaulish village, slumbering in the middle of the river and surrounded by a rough stone wall, until a spring day in 53 B.C. when Julius Caesar, coming from the Amiénois, sought the shortest road to Sens and the Gâtinais.

That spring the Senones and the Carnutes — the tribes from the districts of Sens and Orleans — had refused to send delegates to the assembly of Gaul which was being held in the camp of Amiens. Caesar, regarding this as an act of insubordination, set out with his legions and decided to transfer the Assembly to Lutetia Parisiorum, the village nearest to the rebel territories.

Surmounted by eagles and she-wolves, the standards of the Roman centuries appeared among the willows and reeds which grew on the right bank, near where the Place du Châtelet stands today. The legionaries trampled the mud where on crowded evenings we queue to enter the Théâtre des Nations. Actors in a legendary march, they had come to play the prologue to an epic in twenty acts, covering twenty centuries.

Caesar reined in his horse and, pointing to the island opposite, where conical roofs appeared among the leafy trees, he said: 'I shall set up my camp there tonight.'

In doing so he drew Paris from the shadows, like a winning number in the lottery of history. And by establishing the assembly of Gaul there for a few days, he foreshadowed the part it was to play as a capital city.

Four years later, Caesar became the master of Rome. But he had already, in passing, chosen the city that would one day succeed to Rome.

2 TIBERIUS'S COLUMN

When Caesar left, the tribe of the Parisii rose in rebellion. Labienus, one of Caesar's lieutenants, defeated Camolugenus, a lieutenant of Vercingetorix, in the plain of Grenelle. This battle took place on the site of the present Champ de Mars and the École de Guerre.

Such parallels make one wonder. They seem to imply that the first actions men perform in a given place impregnate it for ever, sowing a seed that will go on yielding a similar harvest for ever.

The Romans set up a permanent garrison at Lutetia. The fortified camp, the castellum, was built on the island. Where Caesar's tent was probably pitched, and Labienus's certainly, the palatium was soon to be built, the Roman prefect's stone dwelling and tribunal where he dispensed justice.

From the time of Augustus, the three Gauls —Belgium, the Lyonnais and Aquitaine— were under the direct control of the Emperors, unlike the Narbonnais, or Provincia Romana (Provence), which was governed by the Senate. Caesar's immediate successors each in his turn travelled through and inspected the three Gauls. First, Augustus made a protracted stay to organise the administrative districts; then Tiberius, whose uneasy memory is recalled by the Triumphal Arch in Orange; and then Caligula, who founded the first literary competitions in Lyons. The Caligula award had something of the same status as the Goncourt. Claudius was born in Lyons, and the Roman Senators amused themselves by calling him a Gaul. Though Nero turned more particularly towards Greece, Galba and Vitellius from necessity took the road to Gaul again in order to suppress the last risings.

At Lutetia, the *nautae* —the watermen and river merchants who, together with the line fishermen, first gave the town its prosperity— dedicated a votive column to Jupiter. It was erected opposite the palatium, on the point of the island, facing upstream. This took place during the reign of Tiberius and at about the same time as the officers of the procurator Pilate in Judaea were arresting a visionary healer whose preaching was disturbing public order. This same Pilate, moreover, was to end his career in Gaul, exiled to Vienne, where it seems he committed suicide; not from remorse, for crucifixion was the normal death penalty inflicted by the administrators of the period, but from despair at having fallen into imperial disfavour. He had no doubt forgotten even the name of the Jew, Jesus of Nazareth.

Jupiter's column stood on the exact site of Notre-Dame. The stone blocks were found in the foundations of the Cathedral's choir during work carried out in the eighteenth century. The column, the most ancient of the capital's monuments, is interesting on more than one count; it bears on its four faces representations not only of the Roman gods but also of the Gaulish deities. An altar for offerings or sacrifices must have stood near by.

Where the palace and the altar stood, the Frankish kings and the Christian cult were to establish themselves. And the boat of the *nautae* was to become the central emblem in the armies of Paris. A town in the shape of a ship, a town on the water and owing its wealth to the water, even its name seems to have been drawn from the river, since it is probably derived from the Gaulish word *par*, which meant boat.

But Lutetia was still far from being the most important Gaulish centre. The Emperor's legate, or the procurator, lived in Lyons. Even in Belgian Gaul the Parisii were of no great account and were administratively subject to the Senones. Later on the Church, as if casting itself in the same mould, divided the religious jurisdictions in accordance with the Roman territorial divisions. This was why the bishopric of Paris, as late as the reign of Louis XIII, was still hierarchically subject to the archbishopric of Sens.

Nevertheless, throughout the first imperial period the town continued to grow and assert itself. The island soon became overcrowded. Too many people wanted to live there; too many activities were being carried on. The problem of expansion was solved by encroaching on the left bank; it was here that the new districts came into being and the new public buildings were erected.

Originally a halt at the crossing of a road and a river, Lutetia was never to forget its function as a stage for travellers and a trading post. It pushed out new roads towards Melun, Meaux and Soissons, towards Pontoise and Rouen, towards Dreux and Chartres, and became the centre of a radical system of communications. It built its future on the

highways along which men carried their ambitions and the produce of
their labours. But the principal road remained Caesar's, the road to Sens
and Orleans, which was so much frequented that it soon became
necessary, in order to avoid traffic jams, to build a relief road parallel to
it, the *via inferior* popularly known as the *via infer*, which in the Middle
Ages became the *Rue d'Enfer*, and then, by a last historical play on
words, the Rue Denfert-Rochereau.

The first burgesses of Paris whose names we know were called
Marcellus, Tetricus, Serdus and Solimarus. In the mornings, they went
to the baths on the site of which the Musée de Cluny stands today.
Sitting in the steam bath, they discussed business or politics, and talked
of the latest news from Rome. They approved the energetic measures
taken by the legate of the Emperor Marcus Aurelius to counter Christian propaganda at Vienne and Lyons. If some question of trade or
transport had to be arranged, or some lawsuit decided, they went to the
island, to the prefect's palace which was the seat of the administration
and where justice was dispensed. Sometimes a touring circus with a
menagerie, jugglers and prize-fighters would give performances in the
town. Here — Jupiter be praised — there were as yet no Christians to
throw to the lions; but there were famous gladiators to play the star
parts. Serdus and Solimarus, Tetricus and Marcellus would go to the
arena (in the neighbourhood of the Rue Monge) and occupy their stone
seats; they owned them and their names were engraved on them.
Indeed, this is how we know of them. On summer days, they would go
to the theatre which, near the present Rue Racine, was cut out of the
slope of the Place de l'Odéon, the first Paris theatre where only matinées
were performed. Seneca, Terence and Plautus were acted; *Phaedra* was
acted. Tetricus, Solimarus, Serdus and Marcellus, Gallo-Roman
burgesses, lived in the Latin Quarter.

3 DENIS'S PREACHING

There is a thousand-year-old tradition that Paris entertained its first
revolutionary before the end of the first century A.D. He was called
Dionysius or Denis. Born in Athens, he had been profoundly impressed
in his youth by the eclipse that had darkened the whole of the eastern
Mediterranean on Good Friday. Converted by Saint Paul when he

visited Greece to recruit disciples, Denis founded the first Athenian church before going to Rome at the time when Nero had imprisoned Peter and Paul on charges of lawbreaking, association with malefactors and arson; finally he was sent to Gaul by Clement, Peter's third successor, to evangelise the Paris region.

A more careful reading of Gregory of Tours, the ancestor of all French historians, makes it clear — alas, alas! — that Dionysos, the first Bishop of Athens, and Dionysius, the first Bishop of Paris, were not the same man. It was too good to be true. One hundred and fifty years separated them, and we are obliged to discard this happy thought. The foundation of the bishopric of Paris dates from the period of the Emperor Decius, about the middle of the third century, and not from the reign of Domitian.

Nevertheless, Denis the Parisian came from Rome, was probably Greek and in any case nurtured on Hellenism, as were the Evangelists. Since the island was the seat of the official religion, and Christianity was under an interdict, Denis taught his philosophy of liberty, equality and fraternity in the suburbs of the left bank on the fringe of the country-side. He did not, properly speaking, preach social revolution; but he denied the emperor's divinity, and fought for a Church independent of the State, whose priests would be ministers of the spirit and not magistrates in the service of civil power. The freemen of the region, oppressed by the occupying Romans, the slaves, and even young people of the noble classes attracted by the new morality, flocked to hear his teaching in the crypts. Communal meals, consisting simply of bread and wine, at which the memory of the Master and His Mother were celebrated, were held in a place that has remained dedicated to the cult and was later to be called Notre-Dame-des-Champs.

The Prefect Fescenninus, after reporting to the emperor, had the agitator Denis and his two principal acolytes, Rusticus and Eleutherus, arrested. They were imprisoned in the Glaucia prison on the Quai aux Fleurs. The modern Préfecture of Police stands near by.

After interrogation, Denis and his companions were taken to the north of the town, to the hill on which the Temple of Mercury then stood. The route they took, the straight, flagged Roman road, has retained the name of the Rue des Martyrs.

Three times on the way Denis was urged to recant, his life being offered him in exchange. But as he was ninety, he thought that he had little life left and that it was not worth a recantation. After the third refusal, he and his two deacons were decapitated in front of the temple on top of the hill. From that day Mount Mercury became the Mons Martyrum — Montmartre.

Some phenomenon of collective hallucination must have seized on those present, or perhaps some frenzy of the popular imagination exaggerated their accounts in the telling, for it was reported that they had seen Denis rise from the block, pick up his head with its long white beard, wash it in a nearby spring and continue to walk northwards for six thousand paces. The miracle is that this was believed. The tomb of Saint Denis soon became a holy place, rather like a Moslem shrine. It was said that the fields about it displayed a wonderful fertility. Benedictine monks later established themselves there; and King Dagobert having chosen it as his place of burial, Saint-Denis thenceforth became the royal necropolis.

But Dionysius had given Paris more than a place of pilgrimage or a resting-place for royal bones. He had brought the Greek spirit to this town of Roman law. After him, the left bank was never to cease welcoming philosophers, thinkers, teachers and reformers in search of a deeper knowledge of mankind and a juster morality. And the discussions, to the present day, were to remain Athenian.

4 JULIAN'S CORONATION

In less than a century the new religion had ceased to be persecuted and was more or less officially accepted. Constantine the Great, leaving Gaul in about 312, adopted the Cross for his emblem as he fought his way through bloodshed and massacre to supreme power. He was to go as far as Byzantium, which from then on was called Constantinople. Pitiless to his rivals, the first Christian emperor was not exactly the pious hero honoured by tradition, nor the best example of the virtues of his creed. This all-powerful convert, who attended the Council of Nicaea as 'exterior bishop', nevertheless had his wife, son and father-in-law assassinated — a true family butcher!

As the Christians emerged from the catacombs, they seem to have enlarged those cracks, already appearing in the great Roman edifice, which were to hasten its decline. The empire was too vast; its capital was now in the east; its crown, constantly at auction, was the object of blood-stained struggles between ambitious rivals; it consisted of too many dissimilar nations, and its rapacious armies were composed of too many mercenaries raised in ill-pacified regions. Immense racial migrations moving ever closer across eastern Europe from Asia, were beating like a flood tide against the frontiers of the Danube and the Rhine; and within the Empire itself minds were now divided between two religions, the old which tolerated all others, and the new which excluded every rival.

It seemed as if the God of the Christians were kindling the fires of punishment on every hand. When Rome burned, at the time of Nero, the disciples of Peter and Paul cried joyfully that divine vengeance was falling upon the city, the new Babylon, the universal seat of sin. But what had little Lutetia done to deserve so great an affliction? For it too was ravaged by the flames. Fire destroyed all the fine left bank; and since the times were no longer prosperous, since commerce, whether by road or river, had diminished because of the general insecurity, the movement of troops, the levying of men, sedation, wars between pretenders to the Empire and threats of invasion, nothing was rebuilt. The people preferred to plant vines about the ruined baths and burntout temples. The population crowded on to the island, into the Cité, and the houses grew taller.

Though property and profits had diminished, taxes were far from doing so. It is not only in recent times that Parisians have cursed the inland revenue and its agents. Of the great Roman administrative bodies there was none more active and efficient, indeed over-efficient, than the tax-collectors who oppressed the country and, adding to all its many afflictions, reduced it to the greatest distress.

In February 358 a messenger of hope arrived in Lutetia. He was twenty-five. His name was Julian and he bore the title of Caesar which, since Diocletian, had designated the recognised heir to the imperial throne. The names of Julian (or Julius) and Caesar, now combined for the second time after a lapse of four hundred years, were decidedly auspicious for the town. Let us pause a moment to consider the man who was, as it were, the second founder of Paris. His memory deserves it.

Flavius Claudius Julian Caesar, nephew of Constantine the Great and cousin of the Emperor Constantius II — who was also his brother-in-law since, for reasons of state, he had had to marry Constantius's sister, Helen — was the only survivor of a family of which no member ever died of old age and few of disease: fratricide, infanticide, parricide and the murder of relatives and friends were their common practice. To remove potential rivals for the throne, the sons of Constantine had killed off all their relations. Constantius was their final victor in this hecatomb of which Julian was the sole survivor.

The imperial power was none the less threatened, for there were many who had an eye on the succession and some who were not even prepared to wait until the way was clear. This was the period of proclamations; every army commander, if he was something of an adventurer, might hope to be proclaimed by his troops, and the greatest battles of the century were fought between the emperor and his generals. A German officer, Magnentius, donned the purple at Autun and seized power in Gaul and the west, thereby obliging Constantius to hurry from Constantinople, defeat him in Pannonia and pursue him as far as Lyons. And a Frankish chief, Silvanus, commander of the infantry, having been invested more recently with the dignity of Emperor, ruled for twenty-eight days around Cologne.

Julian had spent his youth under surveillance in various parts of Greece and Italy. Although he had been brought up in the Christian faith, he soon rejected it to return with enthusiasm to the practice of the ancient cults. Was he impelled towards them by the noble examples of charity and neighbourly love afforded by his family? Or by disgust at the conflicts and intrigues that divided the clergy of the new religion, in which schisms already flourished and every man accused his neighbour of heresy? What is most probable is that, imbued with the Hellenic philosophy which he had studied deeply during his periods of exile, Julian returned to the religion improperly called pagan, as to the highest expression of this philosophy. Moreover, from a political point of view, he saw in Christianity a principle that was contrary to the fundamentals of the Roman 'imperium' and therefore fatal to its conversation.

Julian's memory suffers even today from the sinister cognomen of Apostate, maliciously given him by the first historians of the Church. The title of Restorer would have been more fitting.

This young man, more given to letters than instructed in the military arts, who wrote epigrams, pages of memoirs, an essay on dogma and odes to the sun in the course of his campaigns, drove the Alamani from the Vosges to Cologne during his first year of command, although he very nearly perished in Sens when surprised by a large body of Alamani who had advanced thus far to besiege the town. In the second year he won the decisive victory of Strasbourg, where he crushed both the

Franks and the Alamani and drove them from the left bank of the Rhine which they were holding in strength.

It was a strange period in which one can no longer draw the line between peoples, powers or consciences! The Frankish tribes were among the invaders; but the units which repulsed them also consisted largely of Franks. And there was the barbarian invasion, due less to the barbarians themselves than to the Emperor Constantius, who opened the road to Gaul to them to put an obstacle in the way of his rebellious generals. But when the barbarians responded to the invitation with too much success Constantius ordered Julian to drive them back. Did he hope for their defeat or for that of his designated heir? Julian discovered that some of his officers were betraying his orders hoping thereby to please the Emperor.

However, in the end Julian Caesar was victorious over both enemies and friends. Gaul regained its frontier on the Rhine, as in the happy days of Augustus and Trajan. The posts were held by loyal garrisons.

Prosperity returned to the countryside and, with it, security. Julian moved his government into the *civitas Parisiorum*, just as Caesar had set up the Assembly of Gaul there, and for the same reasons.

For Parisians, the fear of invasion from the east dates from this period. The Alamani had reached a point twenty-five leagues from Lutetia, and its citizens welcomed with gratitude the lettered prince who had saved them from so near a threat. Julian proved himself as wise in administration as he was in battle. He stopped the abuses of the tax collectors and succeeded in reducing taxation by two-thirds, and from then on Gaul could not sing his praises loud enough.

Once again the inhabitants of Lutetia fished from the river-banks while the *nautae* plied upstream and down, their boats laden with grain, wine, wool and leather to be unloaded into the warehouses; and once again building stone was quarried from Mont Parnasse and the valley of the Bièvre.

Julian stayed in Paris three years, or rather three winters, between his campaigns and tours of inspection. He spent his days in government and a great part of his nights writing, in a deliberately unheated room.

Later, he was to write nostalgically: 'I was in my dear Lutetia, for thus is the town of the Parisians called in Gaul. It occupies an island in the middle of the river; wooden bridges link it to the two banks. The river rarely rises or falls; as it is in summer, so it is in winter; the water is pleasant to drink, for it is very pure and agreeable to the eye...'

He praised the mild climate, although one day from the windows of the palatium he saw ice-floes on the Seine 'drifting in like marble paving-tiles'; he appreciated the quality of the vines and the art the Parisians had of growing fig-trees by wrapping them in wheat-straw like a garment to protect them from the inclemency of the seasons.

Paris was quick to forget Julian's benefactions, and even his name. But, as a child will remain marked for life from having lived for a while with a wise, powerful and wealthy relative, so Paris was to remember unconsciously having been for three years the real seat of the Roman Empire of the west; its nerves remained those of an administrative centre and its attitude that of a capital city.

But Byzantium was growing perturbed by Julian's widespread, increasing popularity. To weaken him they first removed his principal assistant and most loyal friend, the Quaestor Sallust, a Gaul. Then a legate from the Emperor, issuing orders without reference to the Caesar, proposed to withdraw half his armies in order to send them to the east. The population was panic-stricken at the thought of being again left defenceless against invasion. They thronged round the legionaries in the streets, beseeching them to stay; and as they marched past women held out their children to the soldiers, who in many cases were their fathers.

There was much dissatisfaction in the army, particularly among the units of Germans and Franks, who had enrolled on condition that they would not have to cross the Alps. From a tribune erected on the Champ de Mars, where the troops under marching orders had been assembled for a final parade, Julian did his best to calm the men; but the more he exhorted them, counselled obedience, and listened with understanding to their grievances, the more furious did they become at being torn from so good a commander. That night, riots broke out. The mutinous soldiers seized their arms and surrounded the palace, shouting: 'Julian — Augustus! Julian — Augustus!' And 'Julian Augustus' meant 'Julian Emperor'.

Men who accede to great positions in the state are given to protesting that they have yielded to the pressure of their friends and to the claim of duty. For once, it was true. Never was a prince faced with a more explicit and immediate choice between supreme power and death: for the soldiers would certainly have killed him had he betrayed them by refusing.

All the same Julian hesitated all night, meditating before an open window, asking Jupiter, 'master of kings and of the planet which distributes power', to guide his decision. Did that window give on to the column of the *nautae*? Next morning, he emerged from the palace. Thousands of voices demanded his answer. Once again, he tried to calm the troops, assuring them that he would obtain on their behalf the Emperor's understanding and clemency. But they wanted no other emperor but Julian. They chaired him on an infantryman's shield. For the first time a Roman Emperor was hoisted on a shield, in the Frankish manner. And this took place on the very site of the precinct of Notre-Dame.

Since no diadem could be found with which to crown Julian, it was suggested to him that he should borrow his wife's tiara. Julian refused to begin his reign wearing a woman's ornament. Someone else suggested that a piece of silver gilt harness decorating the chest of an officer's horse should be used. 'I do not want a horse's ornament either,' Julian replied. In the end, the gold collar with which a standard-bearer had been decorated—the collar in effect of an order—was tied about his forehead.

The same troops who had so violently refused to leave set out rejoicing with him for Constantinople in July 360. The two Emperors, one coming from Lutetia, the other from Syria, where he had been putting down a rebellion, were moving to meet other each when Constantius died, naming *in extremis* his rival as his legitimate successor. Julian lived for another two years and died on his return from a lightning campaign against the Persians, having been mortally wounded when crossing those same deserts of Asia Minor which had been so disastrous for Alexander the Great. He was thirty-one years old. His fate proved the rule he made for himself: 'It is better to do well for a short time than ill for a long one.'

Paris, forgetful Paris, where is the monument, the statue, the square dedicated to the memory of your first emperor, your first 'well beloved', the young man who came to you from Byzantium, saved you from invasion, made you his seat of government and was proclaimed within your walls? This 'pagan' prince was better, wiser, cleverer and more humane than many cruel Christians.

Nor can distance in time excuse such faithlessness of memory. Scarcely ninety years separate Julian Caesar from Saint Geneviève, fewer than have elapsed between the war of 1870 and today.

5 AETIUS'S VICTORY

Paris had had its conquering founder, its revolutionary saint, its first uprising and its first emperor. It was now to have its first prophetess and its first saviour.

Since Julian's death, and still more since that of the Emperor Theodosius (395), the barbarians had reappeared. They were not quite the anarchic hordes, the primitive plunderers, we tend to imagine. The term 'barbarians' obscures the fact that they had kings and laws, rules of inheritance, penal customs, handicrafts if not yet industries, representative assemblies and advanced military training; and these were continually being altered or improved by contact with Roman institutions.

As we have seen, many barbarians had taken service in the imperial armies; many others had been installed, as farmers or as slaves, by the great Gallo-Roman landed proprietors.

But now it was the whole peoples who sought to establish themselves, and with a surprising sense of 'regional economy', as our experts would express it today — that it to say, with an eye to road and river communications, centres of urban activity and natural resources.

The Visigoths, after devastating Greece and Italy, had finally established themselves in Aquitaine, with Bordeaux and Toulouse as their principal cities. But their king, Ataulf, though he had taken and pillaged Rome in passing, now proclaimed himself defender of the greatness of Rome as the heir to its emperors. Had he not married the sister of Honorius, daughter of the great Theodosius?

Part of the Alaman tribes had settled in Alsace. The Burgondes were to leave their name to Burgundy before settling mostly in Savoy. And while the Saxons were seeking settlements on the coasts of the North Sea and the Channel, the Franks, from the lower Rhine, the Meuse and the Sambre, were continually spreading south.

None of these peoples were anarchic in themselves. But, since they fought each other, they brought anarchy and confusion to Gaul. Usurpers, emperors by chance, sprang up in Brittany or Mainz, and the purple clothed the most unexpected shoulders. The only person who had no thought of donning it was the man who, by his authority, lucidity and exceptional energy, would have been worthy of it, the Roman general Aetius. For nearly twenty-five years, sometimes fighting the barbarians, sometimes negotiating and sometimes allying himself

with them, he struggled to maintain some sort of unity in Gaul, and
to preserve the principal centres of its arts and industries, to give it
intervals of precarious peace in which to draw breath and repair its
disasters. It was he who settled the Burgundians in Savoy and
Switzerland, set limits to the expansion of the Goths, halted the Frankish
King Clodio on the banks of the Somme and drove him back into the
Tournaisis.

And what of Paris meanwhile? Paris trembled. Although she was
under the protection of Aetius, ceaselessly fighting or negotiating on the
circumference of a circle, sometimes large and sometimes restricted, of
which Paris, the seat of the administration, was the centre, she nevertheless had good reason to tremble. If the barbarians had invaded Gaul
in such numbers and diversity, if was because they were driven by the
savage pressure of the Hunnish hordes.

Originally consisting of independent tribes, the Huns had recently
found a leader who had succeeded in imposing his suzerainty over them.
They called him Attila, which means 'little father'. History knows him
by no other name.

This violent Asiatic had political ability, and the terror he inspired
was part of his tactics. Having considered attacking the Eastern Empire,
he prefered to turn towards Rome, of which he proclaimed himself the
friend and defender. He proposed to take the sister of the Emperor
Valentinian III as his seven hundred and fiftieth wife, and he assured
the ambassadors that he wished to enter Gaul merely to fight the
Visigoths. There may have been some truth in this, for it seems that
Attila had a personal or ancestral account to settle with the Gothic tribes.

In the early spring of 451, the Huns, their ranks swollen by a horde
of Alamani, crossed the Rhine near Worms, south of Mayence. The
last of their great halting-places was Cologne, which they reduced to
ashes, and it is said that they massacred eleven thousand virgins. Horror
propaganda spread far and wide ahead of them.

On 6 April, Metz was in flames; they were reported to have reached
Verdun, then Laon, Saint-Quentin, Rheims and finally the Marne.
Refugees from the east and north flocked in long columns to the
bridges of Lutetia, blocking the streets in which they camped, before
crossing the other arm of the river. The Roman administration moved
out and retreated to Orleans, then to Tours and then to Aquitaine,
where the Visigoths, faced with imminent danger, suddenly made
common cause with the officials of the Empire in defending the soil of

Gaul. It is not only in modern times that a panic-stricken government
has taken to the road to Bordeaux.

The Parisians, in their terror, began loading their household
belongings on to solid-wheeled wagons. Lutetia was preparing for the
exodus.

And at this point a girl of fifteen, an orphan who, with two friends of
the same age, had founded the first convent in the neighbourhood of
Notre-Dame, began tramping the streets and exhorting the population
to stay. The emaciated Geneviève, who burned with the fires of faith
and carried fasting to the point to denying herself even barley and beans,
cried: 'Go on your knees and pray! I know it, I see it. The Huns will
not come.'

The first miracle, for her too, was that she was believed. The Parisians went on their knees and intoned psalms.

The second miracle was that Attila did not come. But this was easier
to explain. Since he was in fact concerned with the Visigoths, Attila
advanced by the shortest route on Orléans, in the direction of Aquitaine,
intending to take Paris later: rather as Hitler, in 1940, advanced on
Paris instead of pressing on to take London. It was the same kind of
sudden error of strategy and judgement.

Aetius, who had just returned from Italy, assembled all the troops he
could and on 24 June fell on Attila's army, which was besieging Orléans,
just as the town was about to fall. The Hunnish hordes from the Asian
Steppes, with only eighty leagues to cover before reaching the Atlantic
Ocean, were dumbfounded at being attacked, since they were
accustomed to see the peoples of Europe fly before them. They
retreated.

Peril is a great promoter of union, and Aetius was a great general,
Circumstances made him the man of the moment. He returned to Paris.
brought back the administration, and spent three months rallying all the
tribes of Gaul, the most ancient and the newest. Had Attila invaded the
whole valley of the Seine, the Franks could never have united and
the coalition would undoubtedly have been impossible.

On 20 September, at the head of an army come from the four points
of the compass, in which Visigoths, Armoricans, Franks and Burgundians marched with the Gallo-Roman troops, Aetius again attacked the
Huns on the Champs Catalauniques, in the plain that lies between
Châlons and Troyes.

The battle, which lasted three days, was vast, furious and the most decisive in all history and one of the most murderous. Attila, barricaded behind his chariots, was prepared to have himself burnt on a pyre of harness and booty, rather like Hitler in his bunker. But he managed to escape under cover of darkness and retreated across the Rhine with what troops remained to him. He attacked northern Italy again in the following year, and died suddenly in 453, during his seven hundred and seventieth or eightieth bridal night, in the arms of a lady named Ildico. Thus ended, in a happy enough fashion, the man who was called 'the scourge of God'.

Aetius died in 454, assassinated by Valentinian III who, as stupid as he was unjust and ungrateful, thus deprived the Empire of its last bulwark.

In 455 the Vandals and their king, Genseric, entered Rome. Twenty years later the Germanian Odoacer had himself proclaimed king of Italy, and the court of Byzantium was officially informed that there was no longer a Roman emperor in the west.

The statue of Geneviève, the patroness of Paris, stands in its stone slenderness on a bridge across the Seine, and the saint's name has spread from chapel and street to a whole hill. The cult is a justified and worthy one; but where is the statue that should remind us of Aetius? What stele or plaque has been dedicated to the first liberator of Gaul? Without the general's efforts, the saint's prayers might well have been less effective.

Aetius has been called 'the last of the Romans'; he might with equal truth be called 'the first of the French'. The alphabet of France's independence begins with that capital A.

The king of the Salian Franks, who fought beside Aetius on the Champs Catalauniques, was called Meroveus.

Chapter 2

The Capital of the Franks

1 CLOVIS'S DECISION

GENEVIÈVE was still alive when, forty years later, Meroveus's grandson, Clovis — or Clodowig, or Ludwig, that is to say Louis — cast an acquisitive eye on Paris from his temporary capital at Rheims.

Elected king of the Salians at the death of his father Childeric, Clovis, between his fifteenth and twenty-fifth year, had established his dominion over all the Frankish tribes from the mouth of the Scheldt to the sources of the Saône, and from the bay of the Somme to the banks of the Moselle; moreover at Soissons he had defeated the principal adversary of the Franks, the adventurer Syagrius, who boasted the strange title of 'King of the Romans', and whose unstable states extended from the Somme to the Loire. Being master of the ancient imperial province of Belgica Secunda and what is today the northern half of France, Clovis thought, logically enough, that the Parisii should come under his sway.

But Geneviève, again embodying the spirit of resistance, and hallowed by the memory of her 'victory' over the Huns, exhorted her fellow citizens to fight the barbarian, pagan and idolatrous Frank. She sustained morale, directed the defence, and, between two onslaughts, went with eleven barges as far as Arcis-sur-Aube and the district of Troyes to fetch supplies. She seems indeed to have been in command of Lutetia at this time.

But although she had been able to withstand Attila because Attila had not come, and more recently had added to her glory by securing the repatriation of a number of prisoners from Clovis's father while Childeric was at grips with Syagrius, this time she was finally obliged to submit to Clovis, and the city surrendered.

When the early chroniclers reach this painful episode, they tend to become vague or to skate carefully round it. We therefore know almost nothing of the matter of Geneviève's failure, nor of her conduct as a warrior. We may suppose, however, that Clovis showed her no particular clemency.

Three years later, possibly for love but certainly for political reasons, Clovis married the haughty Clotilde, niece of the King of the Burgundians, who was a Christian.

Hope at once revived in Geneviève, who was always attracted to difficult tasks. She had been unable to repulse the Frank with arms; now she would besiege his soul with prayer. Everything suggests that she quickly made friends with Clotilde and that together they worked for the King's conversion.

Certainly, Geneviève was as worthy to enjoy so exalted a friendship as she was to direct a royal conscience. Her reputation for valour, asceticism and piety had spread far and wide throughout the world. Indeed, it is said that, shortly before his death, Saint Simeon Stylites, from the summit of the column on which he had lived for twenty-two years near Antioch, called to travellers setting out for the west to carry his greetings to the miraculous woman of Paris who had triumphed over 'the scourge of God'. Such things establish a saint's renown. Moreover, she possessed the power of curing those afflicted with neurosis or hysteria, who were as numerous in those times as in all others; and her influence was increased thereby.

Though violent in war and summary in judgement, Clovis was fairly tolerant in religious matters. From the earliest years of his reign he had appointed prelates, such as Bishop Remi, among his counsellors. He wished to conciliate the Church and proved, in the Soissons affair, that he attached more importance to a sacred vessel than to a soldier's life.

Clotilde persuaded Clovis to have their first-born ceremoniously baptised. Unfortunately, the child died almost at once. A second son, who was also baptised, fell seriously ill. Clovis began to form a poor opinion of the protective virtues of the Christian faith. Then somewhere between Bonn and Mainz, although not at Tolbiac as is usually suggested, his armies wavered when fighting the Alamani. Superstitious like all conquerors, he uttered his famous invocation, 'God of Clotilde!'—and in the course of the day defeat was turned to victory.

Clovis has often been compared, and in particular by Gregory of Tours, to Constantine the Great.

Like Constantine, Clovis became converted, or asserted that he was converted, on the battlefield, making a sort of bargain with the Almighty; like Constantine, he at once became the protector as well as the protégé of the bishops; and again like Constantine, he sought pretexts for war and displayed an insatiable cruelty towards his adversaries, rivals and relations. And behind him, as behind Constantine, the episcopate advanced, distributing absolution and, crozier in hand, consolidating the gains of the Church. The example of the great Emperor, revered by all Christians, must clearly have obsessed Clovis.

The Alaman tribes having made their submission, Clovis, directly he had been baptised by Saint Remi, attacked his Burgundian family-in-law. Though he did not succeed in annexing the kingdom, he at least limited its expansion.

Then he turned again on the Visigoths, against whom he declared a genuine religious war. He crushed them at Vouillé in 507, killing King Alaric II with his own hand, and seized the whole of their territories north of the Pyrenees.

To match his Roman model it only remained for him to kill off the members of his own family. He had begun the process before he was baptised, and he continued it afterwards until they were exterminated. By his orders, every leading member of the family was murdered.

One day he was heard to complain in the Assembly that he was like a traveller among strangers, with not a single relation to turn to in case of need. He did so merely to make sure that he had forgotten none of them. No distant cousin, if any remained, cared to claim so dangerous a kinship. The bishops told the people that the removal of Clovis's enemies one after the other was a sign of God's peculiar favour. After each murder, Clovis built a church. He built a great many.

The prestige of Roman institutions was still so great that, after the war against the Goths, Clovis felt it an honour to accept the insignia of a consul of Rome, and did so at Tours in 508 by decree of the Byzantine Emperor Anastasius.

Shortly afterwards, he summoned a council at Orleans which confirmed the clergy in its privileges.

Thus, in the guise of the defender both of Roman tradition and the Christian faith, the former barbarian, the chief of a Salian tribe now clothed in the consular purple, probably preceded by lictors and certainly escorted by priests, made his triumphal entry into Lutetia. There, as the imperial prefects had done, he established his seat of government.

Once again, it was a decision determined by Lutetia's geographical position. As the centre of a network of communications, the town was well situated for keeping the Franks in the north and recent conquests in the south under surveillance. Doubtless tradition also played a part. Having been chosen both by Caesar and Julian, Lutetia, now selected for the third time, was confirmed in its function of capital city.

It was in Lutetia that Clovis was to live during the last three years of his life; and it was from Lutetia that he administered a kingdom larger than modern France: for although Burgundy and Savoy were lacking, belonging as they did to the Burgundians, as well as Provence and the Narbonnais, which formed part of the Italian Ostrogoth state, the kingdom in the east extended along the Weser and stretched as far as the Danube.

No doubt Clovis was intending to enlarge his kingdom still further when his death, at the age of forty-five, put an end to his dreams of conquest.

A detestable character, a great adventurer and a remarkable politician, Clovis was one of those men chosen by fate to bring his times forcibly to bed of the fruits they must bear. For them it makes no matter whether the mother dies or the child is deformed: it must be born.

There was no other Imperial prefect or Roman consul after Clovis, and the Gauls and Gaulish provinces were spoken of only in the past. From then on Gaul was called the kingdom of Francia, and Lutetia changed its name, to be known henceforth only as Paris.

2 GENEVIÈVE'S TOMB

Geneviève had lived to see all these things come to pass. The longevity of this active and visionary ascetic is clearly remarkable and compels respect. She was still alive in 507, when Clovis and Clotilde, probably in thanksgiving for the victory of Vouillé, laid the foundations of a church, Saints-Apôtres-Pierre-et-Paul, on a hill on the left bank, from which the potters, in Roman times, had extracted their clay; and still alive, and nearly ninety, when in 511 Clotilde had Clovis entombed in the crypt of the new church.

In the following year, during the rigours of winter, Geneviève died, and the people of Paris went into mourning for their aged saint and first resistant, who had somehow become the ancestor of them all. Her remains were placed next to those of Clovis, as if the two former adversaries, being reconciled, were to remain inseparable in death.

The names of Peter and Paul belonged to the whole of Christendom; that of Geneviève only to Paris. The church of the apostles soon became known as the church of Sainte-Geneviève, and an abbey was attached to it.

First rebuilt under Philippe-Auguste, the Abbey Church of Sainte-Geneviève was reconstructed a second time under Louis XV, as the result of a vow he made during an illness. The necessary funds were acquired by increasing the price of lottery tickets. The architect, Soufflot, was given the commission, but died before it was finished.

The brand-new building had scarcely been completed when the Revolution swept in, broke open Geneviève's shrine and dispersed the dust of her thousand-year-old bones to the winds. Her remains were replaced by Mirabeau's heavy carcass. For it was on the occasion of Mirabeau's death that the church, which was used for the burial 'of Frenchmen illustrious by their talents, their virtues, and their services to the country', became the Panthéon.

But Mirabeau no longer rests there. The Constituent Assembly put him there, the Convention removed him to make way for Marat, and Thermidor expelled Marat in his turn. Such is the fate of mausoleums! The last half-century has seen and wondered at a similar reshuffling of remains in the Red Square.

Napoleon returned the Panthéon to religion; Louis-Philippe restored it to the service of fame. Becoming once more the church of Sainte-Geneviève during the Second Empire, it was decked out with church furniture; but this was removed by the Third Republic which re-engraved on its pediment the revolutionary inscription: 'To great men...'

Each wave, Jacobin, imperial, bourgeois and anti-clerical, has deposited there some of its more illustrious jetsam, from Rousseau to Jaurès, from Voltaire to Zola. General Marceau, Marshal Lannes and Admiral de Bougainville are cheek by jowl with the Deputy Baudin, shot on his barricade, and the two Carnots, one a member of the Convention and the other a President of the Republic who was assassinated; and there too lies Gambetta's heart. But what are the banker Perrégaux and the minister Crétet doing in this company? They must have been very eminent at the time of their death. There is decay even in the Panthéon.

The history of the first church of Sainte-Geneviève is the history of the beginnings of Paris; the history of the Panthéon is that of the last two centuries of France.

When, in May 1885, a pauper's hearse, escorted by a crowd such as rich men never attract, came to a halt before the white steps, it brought yet another ancestral figure, the most French of all great poets, Victor Hugo, author of *Les Misérables*, of *La Légende des Siècles* and *Les Châtiments*; he who had cried, when disaster was again approaching from the east and the enemy making camp at Le Bourget, Choisy-le-Roi and Bougival:

'Paris is the city of cities, the city of men. Paris is one great haven of welcome... Is such a capital, a home of light, a centre of intellect, heart and soul, a core of universal thought, to be violated, broken, overwhelmed—and by a barbaric invasion? It cannot and it shall not be. Never, never, never!'

Surely this cry was the reverberating and magnified echo, resounding across thirteen centuries, the voice of Geneviève.

In the Middle Ages pilgrims flocked at all seasons to the relics of the saint; today, from all over the world, pilgrims of the mind come all the year round to file past the poet's ashes. The giant of the word could lie nowhere but beneath that giant dome. For the whole world, the Panthéon is now the tomb of Victor Hugo.

City of cities, city of men; capital and core of thought... Such indeed is the definition of a capital city, which from the days of Clovis Paris has never ceased to be. The central power might absent itself; it might be on holiday in Blois, or represented or in exile at Versailles; and Bourges, Bordeaux and Vichy were to be capitals in defeat. Paris was to remain the capital of all striving, every storm and in every triumph. Nothing great or lasting can take place in France without her participation and her resolve. Clovis's decision sealed her destiny.

3 CHILDEBERT'S ROOF

Rome was no more, and Paris had scarcely begun.

In that night, or rather in that misty dawn that was the early Middle

Ages, cities were seeking their shape, populations their place, and societies their laws.

We cannot say who was the second king of France. There was none, or there were four.

The eldest did not succeed among the Franks. Clovis's sons, Thierry, Clodomir, Childebert and Clotaire, carved up their father's kingdom and shared it as they would have done a private inheritance, a country estate. The names Neustria and Austrasia were invented to describe these divisions; and each brother made himself king in his own quarter of Francia.

Childebert had Paris in his share; but the others, the better to keep an eye on each other and remain as close as possible to the real capital, established their abodes at the very tips of their respective realms, at Soissons, Rheims and Orleans, whence their authority spread in all directions, to the northern banks of the Meuse, the distant heart of Germania and the foothills of the Pyrenees.

Deplorable in every way, especially for sound administration, this system of devolution caused envy, rivalry and implacable hatred which rapidly transformed Merovingian France into the scene of endless crimes. Every death was a welcome opportunity to alter and revise the existing divisions; every infant puling in its cradle was an enemy to be destroyed even before it was weaned. Never did brother pray so devoutly for the death of brother, sister for the barrenness of sister, and it was the dagger, more often than Heaven, that supplied the answer to these prayers.

The proud and pious Clotilde was unable to prevent her two younger sons, Childebert and Clotaire, from murdering the children left by their elder brother, Clodomir. Only one escaped; he took refuge in a monastery and became a monk. His name, first given to a monastery he founded, was passed on to a village, then to a bridge, then to a motorway. His name was Clodoald, and hence Saint-Cloud.

Nevertheless, the kings of the first and second generation retained some sense of the unity of the *Regnum Francorum* and joined together to increase it. They succeeded in annexing the kingdom of Thuringia in Germany, as well as conquering the great kingdom of the Burgundians. They forced the Ostrogoths to cede Provence, and this cession was confirmed by Justinian when he established his dominion over Italy.

At both ends of Europe, it would seem, there were dreams of

reconstructing the Old Roman Empire. There was Theodebert, the most remarkable of Clovis's grandsons, acting from his capital at Rheims with his terrible Frankish and Germanic bands; and at the other end was Justinian of Byzantium, with his Codes, his Institutes and the armies of the great Belisarius.

But the Frankish kings failed beyond the Alps and Pyrenees. Their Alamani generals were defeated in southern Italy and had to evacuate the peninsula. In Spain an expedition under Childebert had no happier fate, and Septimania, the coastal region from the Roussillon to Nîmes, continued to form part of the Visigoth kingdom.

From the sixth century the phrases 'war in Italy' and 'war in Spain' were familiar to the French and already had a ring of ultimate failure.

Childebert brought nothing back from Saragossa but the tunic of Saint Vincent and a gold cross, which came from Toledo. To shelter these pillaged relics, he founded, at the suggestion of Bishop Germain, an abbey on the outskirts of Paris. The site he chose had already been touched by history, for on these same fields Camolugenus had mustered his troops before marching to defeat at the hands of the legions of Labienus on the Champ de Mars.

The new church, first named Saint-Vincent-et-Sainte-Croix, was remarkable for its elaborate mosaics in imitation of those at Ravenna, and still more for its roof, made of sheets of gilded bronze which glittered in the sun.

But his pious expenditure brought no benefit to king Childebert. He died, in 558, on the day after the consecration of the church and was buried in it, as was Bishop Germain eighteen years later.

Because of the bishop and its glittering roof, the Church of Saint-Vincent became popularly known as Saint-Germain-le-Doré; and until the reign of Dagobert it was used as a mausoleum for the kings of the first dynasty. About the year 1000 the roof, having been pillaged by the Norsemen, was replaced by a high square tower with a slate spire on its summit. The whole world knows this church at least by name: for during the last half-century youth from every corner of the globe has gathered in its shadow, in wealth and penury, bringing its boredom and its dreams, its transistors, sports cars, lawless loves and melancholy songs. Childebert's church is Saint-Germain-des-Prés.

4 BRUNHILDA'S EXECUTION

The Frankish Kings now controlled all Western Europe except Iberia and Italy. The frontiers of their dominions stretched from Leipzig to Nice, crossed Bavaria, included Lake Constance and extended along the St Gothard.

Childebert's death, coming after a long succession of deaths both natural and unnatural, enabled Clovis's youngest son, Clotaire, to centralise the government of this immense territory under his own rule; and for three years (558-561), Paris again became the sole capital.

Clotaire's portrait can be only drawn in blood. I need mention but one of his many crimes. When one of his sons sought to make himself independent, Clotaire had him shut up in a wooden hut and set fire to it. This, it would seem, caused him some remorse, and he set out on a pilgrimage of expiation, but went no further than Tours. The following year, having contracted bronchial pneumonia while out hunting, he quarrelled with God and cried indignantly as he lay dying: 'What do you think of a King of Heaven who afflicts the kings of the earth in this way?'

He too left four male heirs; and the Frankish kingdom was again divided into four.

Paris then went through a curious phase which serves to underline her great importance. King Caribert, in whose portion Paris was, was the first to die, and his brothers eagerly divided up his territories between them. But they could not agree as to which should have Paris. In the end, they decided to make it a jointly held city. It was administered by delegated officials, none of the three kings having the right to enter it without the permission of the other two – a state of affairs comparable to that of Berlin after the Second World War.

The strangest thing about this strange treaty is that it was observed for six years; and it is more surprising since one of the signatories, Chilperic, had Fredegonda for mistress, and another, Sigebert, had just married Brunhilda.

There was more to Brunhilda than her appearance in our schoolboy recollections tied to the tail of a horse; she dominated her period. This Visigoth princess had been brought up in Spain in the Roman manner, spoke classical Latin and admired the poets; moreover, she was beautiful, or passed as such since she was a queen. She shines with an unusual lustre in those courts of upstart ruffians and bishops avid for land. She had a grasp of general ideas and political concepts, and qualities of decision, command and perseverance, such as are uncommon in any period, and were particularly so in her own.

Compared with Brunhilda, Fredegonda glowed like a dark gem, or like the eye of a nocturnal carnivore. An uncultivated serf, with no intelligence except ambition, as cruel in victory as she was cowardly in defeat, Fredegonda clearly cannot have lacked animal attraction since Chilperic, to please her, assassinated in the same week his first two wives, one of whom was Brunhilda's sister.

This was the start of the conflict. A little later, Chilperic invaded Sigebert's territories, spreading terror and death. Sigebert replied by throwing his Germanic armies against Chilperic. All treaties were broken. Sigebert made an armed entrance into the jointly held city and installed himself there. Thus Brunhilda became Queen of Paris.

The third brother, Gontran, tried vainly to arbitrate.

The rivalry between Sigebert and Chilperic, and then between their widows and descendants, made history for the next forty years a tale of continuous pillage and massacre. Convents were burned to the ground with all their inmates, assassinations carried out in public or in conjugal beds, kings murdered at the moment of their investiture. Cleverly hollowed daggers from which poison flowed were used, children abducted, hands severed, eyes gouged, fasely sworn loyalties sold to the highest bidder, hatreds handed down as one bequeaths an estate. The worst pages in the annals of Byzantium can show nothing more appalling. Moreover, Byzantium was not entirely innocent of complicity; the Emperor Maurice intervened at one stage in support of the rights of one of Clotaire's bastards.

Sigebert was murdered in Artois and Brunhilda was imprisoned at Rouen. Chilperic was murdered near Paris, and Fredegonda sought asylum in the choir of Notre-Dame. The fortunes, or rather misfortunes, of France were to change sides several more times.

The picture which was eventually drawn by popular memory, and which for many generations appealed to childish sadism, must be somewhat corrected. The truth is even more atrocious than the legend; for vice was rewarded, virtue punished, and old age flouted.

It was not Fredegonda who had her defeated rival put to death. Fredegonda had died sixteen years earlier, after winning a last battle somewhere between Soissons and Laon. She died quietly in the bed she had long shared with her lover, Landeric. Her son, Clotaire II, undertook her posthumous revenge.

Nor was it a beautiful young woman with a generous bosom who was tied to the tail of an unbroken horse, but a grandmother aged seventy-nine. For this was Brunhilda's age. She had reigned with her son, then with her grandsons, then in the name of her great-grandsons. Abandoned, betrayed and arrested, she was accused of crimes covering four reigns, including those committed by Fredegonda. She was tortured for three days, her last descendants being slain before her eyes. Then she was hoisted on to a camel and led up and down amid the laughter and booing of the army. A camel among the Franks! To us this may seem extraordinary; but it merely proves that trade was still maintained with the east and that the Merovingian princes had inherited from Rome a taste for menageries.

Eventually, Brunhilda was tied, by one arm, one leg and her white hair, to the tail of an unbroken horse.

Historians do not agree upon the site of the execution. Most of them, parroting each other, have put it near Dijon; but some say that it took place in Paris, and that the old queen's mutilated body was dragged along what is now the Rue des Petits-Champs. Part of this street, since the last war, has been given the name of a heroine, another woman who suffered execution: Danielle Casanova.

5 DAGOBERT'S THRONE

During the century between the death of Clovis and the reign of the second Clotaire, Paris, though constantly changing hands and kings, never ceased to grow. The parishes were extending on both banks: Saint-Julien, Saint-Séverin, Saint-Merri, Saint-Étienne, Saint-Marcel, Saint-Gervais, Saint-Lazare. Houses huddled round imported relics or the memories of miracle-working priests. We need not be surprised at this flowering of saints, both in Paris and elsewhere, during Merovingian times. Virtue was so rare a commodity that the mere fact of being an honest man, reasonably kindly and generous, was in itself a miracle and deserving of canonisation, by popular consent.

During this period it was really 'only faith alone that saved'; faith — and the clergy who alone could sometimes strike terror into kings.

Paris grew, but in fear and trembling, without order, hygiene or plan. What town-planning was to be expected of a century that could not read and produced, in the whole of the Frankish west, but two writers who can be named: a poet, Fortunatus, who sang the praises of Brunhilda, and the historian Gregory of Tours? No other light burned during this period of decivilisation.

The fratricidal struggles that took toll of the people, as well as killing the kings, are not only evidence of the violence and savagery of manners, but also of the folly of dividing up the state, and of the necessity for a single authority, whose obvious headquarters was Paris.

Brunhilda had been the first to understand this necessity. When her four grandsons became orphans, she had broken with Frankish custom and proclaimed the eldest as sole king. The so-called Salic law whereby the throne passes to the eldest male, relied on so extensively under the last direct Capets, was in fact the decree and invention of Brunhilda, and *contrary* to the Salian code.

Brunhilda's wisdom was of value to her executioner. Clotaire II, the sole survivor of the long family massacre, set about restoring the unity of power. He lived in Paris, where in 614 he summoned an assembly of laymen and a council of bishops; he governed the various Frankish territories by sending them high officers from his household. It was from this time that the function of major or mayor of the Palace became of particular importance, the holders of the office sometimes playing the part of prime minister and sometimes of viceroy. The Mayor of Austrasia, who had been one of the instigators of Brunhilda's trial, was called Pépin; and all the Carolingians were to descend from him.

Clotaire II, who died in 629 and was buried at Saint-Germain-le-Doré, was succeeded by his eldest son, whom Paris was to make the hero of a song: the good King Dagobert, whose minister was the great Saint Éloi.

But the song is not history. On a closer view, the lives of these two men contain surprises.

First, Éloi. His rise was in itself an astonishing performance. He had begun life as a blacksmith at Limoges and was never, it seems, much addicted to modesty, for he had inscribed on his sign: 'Éloi, master of masters, master of all.' In Paris, he set himself up as a goldsmith and soon obtained the custom of the palace to which he supplied cups, dishes, caskets, ciboria and reliquaries. The throne of gilded bronze

known as Dagobert's, and considered his masterpiece, was in fact made
for Clotaire II. Dagobert merely inherited it.

To work in gold, one needs access to the Treasury; and by working
for kings one becomes their counsellor. Éloi had ideas about everything
and a taste for power. On Dagobert's behalf, he reorganised the fiscal
laws and restored the finances. A man of business before he became a
man of the Church, he showed even greater ability as treasurer of the
kingdom that he had as goldsmith to princes.

Ministers of finance are rarely loved. Saint Éloi made himself detested.
Paris hated him. When Dagobert died he hastily left the capital for fear
of assassination. His bishopric of Noyon, where he ended his days, was
a prudent exile. If ever this saint performed a miracle, it was in ex-
tracting so much hard cash from the populace.

As for Dagobert, he was just the opposite of the good man of legend.
If he seemed worthy to be regretted, it was only by comparison with
his successors.

He had the temperament of a warrior, the authority of a despot and
the tastes of a satrap. Assassination was not excluded from his methods
of government. He held marriage vows to be of minor importance and
changed his legitimate wife several times, although this never prevented
him from keeping a hundred or so concubines. If his treasurer caught
him oddly breeched, it was doubtless because he had dressed a little
hastily as he left his harem.

In justice to Dagobert, however, it must be said that by much
travelling, and being well supplied with money by Éloi, he succeeded
where his father had failed and practically restored the unity of the
Regnum Francorum from eastern Germany to the Pyrenees. He was a
brutal but a great king.

In order to contain the Slav peoples, who were beginning to become
active on the frontiers of his Germanic possessions, he concluded a
treaty of friendship and 'perpetual peace' with the Byzantine Emperor
Honorius. That this was possible gives some indication of the extent
of Dagobert's power.

Paris suddenly found herself in the position of being the second city
of the world, at least through the importance of the man who ruled
from her. And the presence of power must attract and encourage every
form of activity, building and trade. It draws the ambitious and is a
magnet to travellers. People must have felt stifled in Paris, deafened by
the noise of her craftsmen in the cramped streets; they must already

have dreamt of the countryside and the open air. And Dagobert enjoyed it staying at his villas at Rueil and Épinay.

It was at Épinay that he died, in 639. His great reign had lasted only ten years. And it was at Saint-Denis, in the church built by Éloi, that he was buried, the first of the kings who were thenceforth to rest there.

After Dagobert, things very quickly disintegrated. Inheritances again divided the kingdom, and even those sovereigns who received Paris in their portion ceased to live in the city. It is never good for the power in France to desert the capital

Were the last Merovingian kings wholly incompetent? Not more so than others. But they had little time to accomplish anything during their short reigns. Often fathers at the age of fourteen or fifteen, the Thierrys, Clotaires and later Dagoberts all died between twenty-three and twenty-five. There were twelve in a hundred years, and their only role was that of a ritual image. They received ambassadors, delivered prepared speeches, signed official documents; orders were sent out in their names; they resigned but did not govern.

These kings could only travel in their coaches at the speed of the oxen that drew them, for there was no other transport. Their mistake was to remain in their villas cut off from the people, preferring a degree of royal pomp, not innocent of debauchery, to the hard task of exercising power. It was their error, and their misfortune, that they did not know how to prevent their high officials, mayors, dukes and counts, from making, unmaking and remaking the kingdom as they pleased, each having the support of a district or a following, until they became virtually independent.

During those hundred years there was only one important and durable foundation in Paris: the Hôtel-Dieu, created by Bishop Landri.

No one at the time, at least in the west, paid heed to a voice that had arisen in the Arabian desert. Busy with their internecine conflicts, the Frankish princes took little account of the marching Bedouins, nor were they seriously aware of their prodigious advance along the Mediterranean.

When Paris at length heard the din of Islam, it was approaching at the gallop from Poitiers. Even then what was mainly heard was the din produced by the Duke of Austrasia, the mayor of the Palace, Charles Martel.

Chapter 3

Forgotten by the Empire

I THE INDIFFERENCE OF CHARLES

IT IS NOT CERTAIN that there was, properly speaking, a 'battle' of Poitiers; there was pillaging of the town's suburbs by the Moslems and a 'clash' on the Tours road. As often happens with conquering troops who have left their bases far behind, owing to the very ease of their advance, the Arabs turned tail at the first serious resistance they encountered. Both victors and vanquished had an interest in magnifying the affair in the accounts they gave of it, the former to glorify their exploit and the latter to excuse their retreat.

Nor is it certain that Charles Martel saved the west on that day from a peril as great, imminent and disastrous as he claimed. His adversaries were not the whole of Islam but merely a party of Arabs and converted Visigoths, less interested in any concerted attempt to dominate Europe than in the settlement of accounts between a rebellious emir and his superior. This invasion, at least to begin with, was more in the nature of a large-scale punitive raid.

On the other hand, it is quite certain that Charles Martel had twice ravaged the south-west of France before the coming of the Arabs; and that the latter only invaded that country because the Duke of Aquitaine applied to them for help against Charles.

Similarly, Charles had already ravaged the valleys of the Seine and the Loire which constituted Neustria, as well as Friesland, Bavaria and the Lyonnais; and later, long after the Moslem withdrawal, he was to ravage Aquitaine for the third time. The terror of Francia at that time was not so much Abd el Rahman as Charles Martel himself.

And when the Saracens reappeared in the valley of the Rhône, it was neither Charles Martel nor his ally the King of the Lombards who halted the new invasion; it dissolved before it was even opposed by the religious dissensions which were already dividing Islam and setting limits to its expansion. Charles had merely to advance into Provence to punish traitors and sequester the property of those citizens of Marseilles who had come to terms with the Infidel.

Nevertheless, his famous 'victory' at Poitiers, cleverly exploited and completed by his 'triumphs' in Provence, enabled him to pose as the protector of Europe and the saviour of Christendom, and even to dispense, when Thierry IV died (in the list of sovereigns this Thierry might well bear the title of 'the Unknown') with the fiction of allegiance to any king.

That Charles Martel did not himself assume the crown was due more to lack of time than of will. This bastard son of the Mayor of the Palace, Pépin II, who had resolved to restore his father's absolute power for his own advantage, was a man of the east, an Austrasian; his capital was Metz and for him the great river was not the Seine, but the Rhine. He ignored Paris, except on one occasion in his youth, when he made war there to defeat his first adversaries. He returned to it only in death, to be buried in Saint-Denis, which is sufficient proof that he was treated as a king.

It is probable that throughout his wars he sought, or came to seek, the re-establishment of the always fragile unity of the Frankish empire, though he had a purely personal conception of this unity and saw it only as an extension of himself, under his own dominion; a unity of power rather than a unity of peoples.

The more determined to defend his rights since his illegitimate birth rendered these questionable, Charles Martel had relied, in his early ventures, on the support of the high officials and great landed proprietors of Austrasia, who saw in him a providential defender of their power and property. He observed this principle throughout his life, and his descendants followed his example, always favouring great wealth and interests, whether ecclesiastical or lay. The landed classes are always ready to support adventurers who will safeguard their possessions. The Carolingian dynasty, more than any other, was to be the monarchy of the privileged.

The Paris crafts and merchandise, transport, commerce and invention, the market-place of produce and ideas with its countless minor trades and few substantial fortunes, could be of no interest to the Carolingians.

2 PÉPIN'S CORONATION

Nevertheless in the ensuing years Paris was to be the scene and witness of political acts that were to affect all the centuries that followed.

The dreams of hegemony entertained by Charles Martel and his government had not cemented the *Regnum Francorum* very solidly, nor been generally accepted by the people. Indeed, his son and successor, Pépin the Short, displaying as much warlike ardour and conducting his campaigns with an equal ferocity, had to lead an expedition into Aquitaine, two into Germania, two more into Italy against the Lombards, former allies of his father, and finally to declare a second war in Aquitaine which lasted eight atrocious years.

When we read the history of Charles Martel, we find the word 'pillage' on nearly every page, but in the history of his son the word is 'devastation'. The devastation of Berry, of Auvergne, of Limousin and Quercy; the devastation of Languedoc; there is something more deliberate and systematic about devastation than there is about casual pillage. Pépin, all historians are agreed, had a more developed political sense than his father.

He was fortunate, moreover, in that his elder brother, Carloman, who had little gift for the exercise of power and was disgusted by the massacres he had witnessed, soon removed himself by entering a religious order. Pépin, the sole master, or rather the sole mayor methodically and systematically set about gaining the throne. While accomplishing this long-drawn operation, he found it convenient to remember Paris.

He did so first in 743, when he caused the last Merovingian, Childeric III, a shadowy phantom of a king, in whose name he was to govern with complete power for eight years, to be proclaimed on the Champ de Mars. At the end of those eight years, having extracted from Pope Zacharius the strange opinion that 'it is better to call king the man who has the power rather than the man who is deprived of it', Pépin summoned to Soissons an assembly which conferred on him, or transferred to him, the royal title, 'by election of all the Franks, the consecration of the bishops and the submission of the great'. Thus the old chronicler expresses it. In this strange referendum it would seem that the votes of *the great* and *the bishops* carried as much weight as those of *all the Franks*. This was, in a sense, a foreshadowing, perhaps even the origin, of the juridical division of the French people into three estates, a division that was to endure till the end of the monarchy.

The last Childeric was tonsured and relegated to the silence of the cloister. To celebrate his accession, the great monasteries received large donations from the new sovereign, raised from the lands and possessions of *all the Franks*.

It must be remembered that the clergy in this rough age had habits which are to us surprising. The bishops were often married, their sons claimed to inherit their bishoprics, abbots robbed their own monasteries to live like lords and indulge in war, hunting and debauchery, priests became moneylenders and many laymen held church livings, as one might own a business or an estate, 'without even going to the trouble of taking orders'.

The papacy, horrified by the state of the Frankish Church, begged Pépin to put an end to these scandals and reform his clergy, which in fact Pépin methodically and systematically set about doing. But the papacy itself was living under the threat of the Lombards.

Pépin the Short then remembered Paris, or rather Saint-Denis, a second time, and offered Pope Stephen II, Zacharius's successor, asylum and residence there.

The encounter between Stephen and Pépin at the beginning of 754 was moving indeed. Pépin went to meet the Pope's retinue, leapt from the saddle, and humbly took the Pope's horse by the bridle. When, however, they had entered the first chapel, it was the Pontiff's turn to throw himself at Pépin's feet and implore his protection. History has sometimes its humorous side; it was the day of the Feast of Kings.

If Stephen could no longer maintain himself in his Roman see, Pépin himself was not too sure of being able to retain his new throne. An election had raised him to it, another might equally well unseat him; it would appear that not *all the Franks* had been properly represented in the assembly at Soissons, nor had they been entirely unanimous; serious disturbances were beginning to take place.

Taking advantage of the fact that the Pope was his guest and under an obligation to him, Pépin had himself crowned by the Holy Father six months later, amid great pomp, in the basilica of Saint-Denis.

Let us pause a moment at this coronation which took place on 28 July 754. It is scarcely mentioned in our school books; and yet its political importance was probably greater than that of Charlemagne. The inhabitants of Paris who gathered on foot that summer's day to to witness the ceremony, were present at an event, an innovation, of which the effects endured until our own times.

In the first place, the nature of Frankish monarchies was altered for ever. No Merovingian had ever been crowned. Even within a tradition of hereditary succession, the public act confering the royal power had been election, which could be reversed, and in fact often was.

The anointing with holy oil was not a Frankish custom, any more than it had originally been a Christian one. It was a rite borrowed from the magic liturgies of Antiquity and, in particular, the Pharaonic. By his anointing the sovereign became the elect, not of men, but of God; his person took on a sacred and intangible character. *Tu es sacerdos in aeternum*. From then on, any act of opposition was akin to sacrilege. This was the origin of the divine right of kings. It is a perfectly tenable system where the State is a theocracy in which the supreme political and religious heads are one and the same; but where the prince and the pontiff are two separate individuals, where dogma and law have different origins, and where temporal and spiritual power are separately exercised, a precarious, uncertain and ambiguous state of affairs must arise in which the two powers are obliged to form alliances of interest or else vie with each other for pre-eminence. The king expects to rule over the clergy, since they are his subjects, and the pontiff over the subjects, even the king, since they are his flock. Unless sovereigns make themselves the first officers of the pope, as did the Carolingians, and the popes make themselves first chaplains to the kings — as did Stephen II and his successors, with the civil power treating the clergy as a privileged class, and the Church covering up the abuses of government — the results must necessarily be deplorable. The Emperor Henry kneeling in the snow at Canossa, or Pope Boniface having his face slapped on his throne at Anagni, are instances. A further alternative is schism, when, like Henry VIII of England, a king takes the harshly logical step of making himself head of his national Church.

The conclaves of Carpentras and of Lyons under siege, the interminable divisions between Gallicans and Ultramontanists, and the dramas, continuing into our own century, occasioned by the seizure of religious property due to the separation of Church and State, were for France the poisoned fruits of Pépin's coronation.

Another consequence of the anointing at Saint-Denis, and one no less disastrous, was the creation of a papal kingdom in Italy.

Strangely, the popes of Stephen's period held themselves to be heirs to the Roman Republic, and claimed every title of authority that had escaped the dominion of the Byzantine Empire. On the day of the coronation, Stephen conferred on Pépin the title of 'patrician of the Romans', a purely honorific dignity which on occasion the emperors, since Constantine, had bestowed on foreign princes. In acting thus, Stephen was not behaving as the representative of Christ, but as the successor to the *pontifex maximus* of the pagan religion. Never had the papacy been further from the teaching of the gospels, or more deliberately confused what was Caesar's with what was God's.

The agreement — one might even say the bargain — between Stephen and Pépin was perfectly clear: 'I will crown you in Paris, and you will restore me to Rome.' Pépin set out for Italy the very next month. Vainly did Carloman, his elder brother, emerge from his monastic retreat at Monte Cassino to implore him to give up his war against the Lombards, ancient allies of the Franks. Pépin was now in a position to ignore every remonstrance; he carried the sword of God. He made use of it with his habitual determination.

Susa was devastated; and the Pope uttered the word 'miracle'. Pisa was devastated; and the Pope compared Pépin to both David and Solomon. When the war appeared to be marking time because the Frankish leaders were tired of it, Pope Stephen immediately began to inveigh and fulminate. He had no compunction about sending Pépin a letter signed 'St Peter', as if the apostle had himself written it in his tomb, in which he summoned the Franks 'to come to the defence of the dwelling where he reposed in the flesh'. And Pépin set out again.

The defeated Lombards abandoned to Pépin the ancient exarchate of Ravenna which included, besides Ravenna itself, a dozen towns such as Rimini, Forli and Urbino. And these territories, still nominally possessions of the Byzantine Empire, were immediately made over by Pépin in perpetuity 'to the Roman Church, St Peter and the pontiffs his successors'. Thus did Pépin pay the price of his coronation; and Fulrad, the abbot of Saint-Denis, was sent to deposit, as a solemn counterpart of his anointing, the keys of these towns on the tomb that was asserted to be that of the first apostle, as well as the deed of gift. The Papal State had been born. The keys of St Peter are in fact those of Pépin.

The Church was to suffer from the unhappy gift for twelve centuries. Having become temporal sovereigns with all that this entailed — alliance or strife with other kingdoms, financial problems, military levies, wars, internal repression, the maintenance of a palace force, capital punishment etc. — the popes saw their moral authority correspondingly decline. The pontifical tiara became, as had the imperial crown in the past, a stake to be played for by every low and earthly ambition. The struggles between popes and anti-popes, between Guelphs and Ghibellines, caused more deaths than the faith had created martyrs. Every heresy, whether Albigensian, Hussite, Spiritual or Waldensian, was a reproach to the papacy for a situation so contrary to Christian teaching; the Reformation was to find this one of its most powerful driving forces.

As late as the middle of the nineteenth century, when Italy was being united, Napoleon III forcibly intervened in favour of the possessions of the Holy See, a last effort to protect Pépin's gift.

It is only during the last hundred years, when the Papal State has been wisely confined to the Vatican — that is to say to the amount of territory necessary to contain the administration of the Church — that the papacy has achieved the universal importance and influence we now acknowledge, which it never possessed before.

Indeed, few actions performed to satisfy the ambition of one man and his clan have had so long a sequel as the first Carolingian coronation.

It was to Saint-Denis that Pépin had himself borne when, having fallen ill on his return from the war in Aquitaine, he felt his end approaching. With his body exhausted by suffering and his mind wholly occupied with the succession, did he cast a glance at the city as he crossed its bridges? Paris for him was only a second city, the residence of the former dynasty, the ancient royal parish close to the family cemetery. He was buried, in conformity with his wish, in that church which contained the bones of all the kings since Dagobert.

Until his last breath, and even with his ashes, Pépin had been concerned to prove that he represented legitimacy. His son, Charlemagne, had no need to worry about this, and so could forget Paris altogether.

3 CHARLEMAGNE'S ABSENCE

The relations between cities and princes are matters of passion rather than of reason. Just as the most pernicious lovers leave their mistresses with the deepest regrets, so, it would seem, do peoples cherish longest the memory of their most disastrous kings. Where their memories are concerned, societies are harlots.

The two sovereigns who in all her history did France the most harm, Charlemagne with his conquest of the west and Napoleon with his European hegemony, are the very two to whose memory the French are most attached and whose names they honour with the greatest constancy. Again like mistresses who, talking of their bad lovers, endow them with qualities they alone could see. ('He ruined me; but what a gentleman he was!' 'He beat me; but what a man!') — so do nations, when they reconstruct their past, embellish their disastrous princes with high virtues they never possessed.

Among all the romantic pictures dished up to the French schoolboy, none is more false, in line and colour, than that of the Emperor Charlemagne.

Since nothing was done in or for Paris during his reign, and since his shadow fills the horizon, let us pause before his bronze statue near Notre-Dame (the only sovereign to be accorded this honour: Philip Augustus has been removed to the Trône gate and Philip the Fair has not a stile, a street or even a blind alley) and gaze at his reflection on the waters of time.

Did I say that societies behave like harlots? Indeed they do, in all senses of the word. For in the masters they submit to, nations in their unhappy passion pursue the search for the father-figure, even the grandfather-figure, the colossus who dominated their childhood, requiring them to find him admirable in all respects, and whose authority, however tinged with deprivation or brutality, was the supreme refuge. The portrait of Charlemagne, the good-hearted, majestic giant with a red beard, it the pure product of popular imagination.

In the first place, he wore no beard, but a long moustache in the Frankish manner spreading across his round face. As for his height, he was certainly tall but not gigantic, and majestic rather in his pot-belly than in his bearing or voice, for the latter was rather piping, and his head was sunk between his shoulders.

He had four legitimate wives. The first, Désirée, was repudiated; the other three died; and when he became a widower for the third time he consoled himself with four concubines. He prevented his daughters marrying, insisted that they should live at home, and preferred to see them populate his court with bastards rather than take husbands.

Nothing in his character displays any particular kindliness, and one searches in vain for the reasons that led an anti-pope in the twelfth century to admit him to the canon of the saints.

Charlemagne ordered the deportation of whole populations. In a single day, and merely on the word of informers, he ordered the execution of four thousand five hundred Saxons whom he was told had taken part in a rebellion. 'That same day,' writes the chronicler, 'they all had their heads cut off. The King, his vengeance satisfied, went into winter quarters at Thionville, where he celebrated the birthday of our Lord, and Easter.'

His methods of evangelising were as summary as his justice; one hundred and twenty *sous* fine for nobles in conquered territory who were not baptised within a year, thirty *sous* for free men, and fifteen *sous* for slaves.

Such was his mania for war that his father and grandfather appear peace-loving in comparison. In the forty-seven years of his reign he conducted at least forty-seven armed expeditions, setting off each year on campaign, as one would go on holiday.

Finally, this patron of schoolboys could not write; he tried it, we are told by his sycophant Eginhard, 'taking the opportunity of moments of leisure to practise tracing letters; but he had begun too late and the result was poor'.

This, in outline, but in true outline, is the portrait of Charlemagne.

His famous remark on coming from the Christmas Mass, in the year 800, at which Pope Leo III placed the imperial crown on his head, while the populace acclaimed him outside St Peter's in Rome – 'Had I known, I would not have entered the church today...' – must not be attributed to modesty, but rather to arrogance, and anger at having been unexpectedly crowned.

For though coronation by anointing, like the 'adoration' with which the ancient Caesars were honoured, was the business of the Pope, the crown belonged to the emperor, who could receive it only from the predecessor who named him his heir, or, failing a predecessor, from himself. These were subtleties, no doubt; but they had their importance, and they bore symbolic witness to the inevitable struggle for supremacy between the civil and religious power.

How did poor Pope Leo, the minor palace official whom Charlemagne had made a pope, come to be mixed up in all this? He could not even maintain himself in his own city, where he was attacked and chastised in the streets. What superiority did he claim by 'making' the Emperor? And what ineptitude: for Charlemagne, whose fourth wife

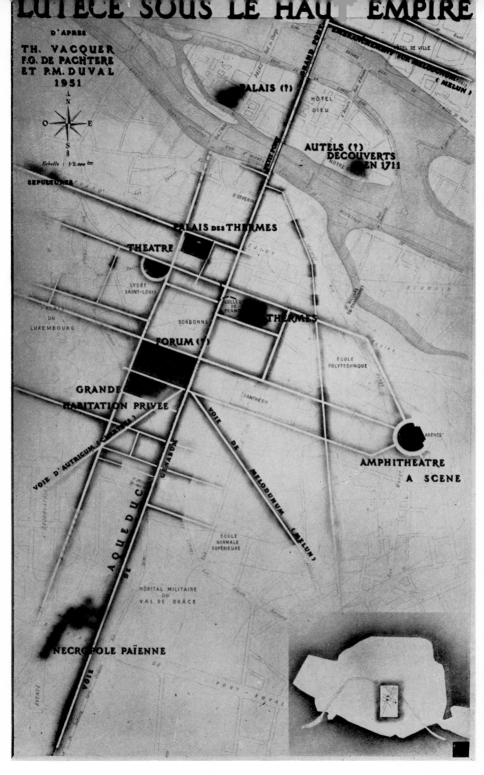

Lutetia in the Early Empire

Charlemagne

Detail of the head of Charlemagne in the Louvre

Corpora de uico quiui nomen modo ſtrata.
Eſt. ſunt tranſ——ra famulatu regiſ amico.
Exit cum plauſu populi deuotio magno.
Et celebratur adhuc proceſſio quilibet anno.

St Eloi offering the crown to Dagobert

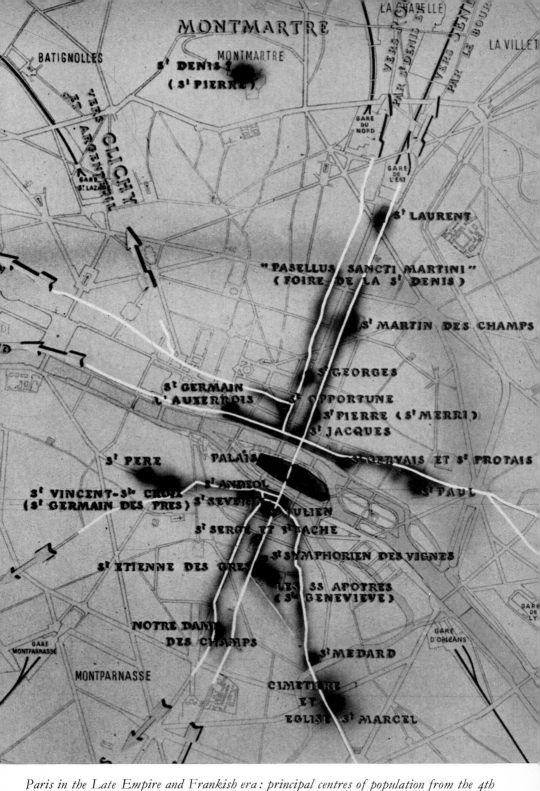

Paris in the Late Empire and Frankish era: principal centres of population from the 4th to the 10th century

Bust of Philippe Auguste

Henri I and Louis VI

Robert II

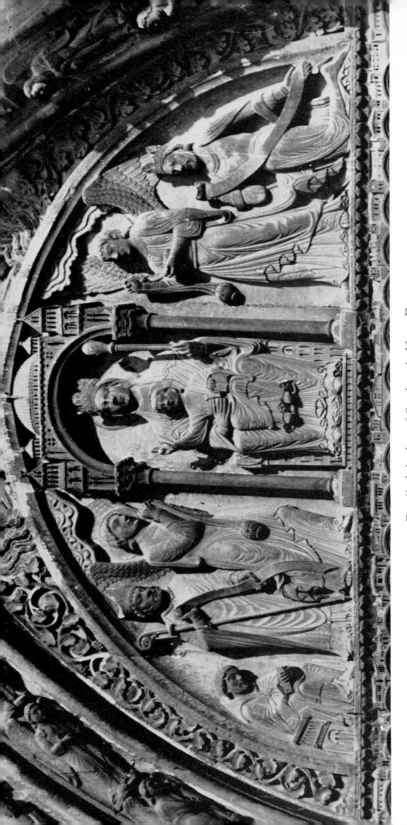

Detail of the door of St Anne in Notre-Dame

aples et monta eulx tous beane
ou ciel se iour de lascention.
Quant le peuple z tous ses
pelerins eurent la este a grans
pleurs za grans prieres. et
que toutes ses priex furent fai
tes sur ses debatz donneulx. Jlz
descendirent du mont de spon
qui est empres la Cite de la
partie de midi au sommet dun
tertre. Les sarrazins qui

estoient sur ses murs et tours
de la ville se merneilloient moult
quel chose noz gens faisoient
Et la ou ilz pouoient veoir
la presse pres deulx se tout
bun arbelestrer ou daultre tout
Jlz y traioient sans cesser. tel
lement quilz en blecerent plu
seurs. et si dressoient cloiv
sur ses murs z traioie noz
gens traioient contre. et

Pope Urban II preaches the First Crusade

Héloïse and Abélard

Du retour en france du roy saint loys. Le xxvme chapitre.
n lay mil CC lij
madame blanche
la royne de france
mere de saint loys qui avoit
la garde z gouvernement

du royaume de france tres
passa de ce siecle z fut por
tee a grant honneur z sole
nite en une eglise de nonais
de lordre de asteaulx nomee

The death of Blanche of Castille

St Louis visiting victims of the plague

Sainte-Chapelle : South-west view

had died six months previously, was looking towards Byzantium and negotiating for the hand of the Empress Irene.

When Napoleon referred to Charlemagne as 'my illustrious predecessor', he made no mistake. Charlemagne was Napoleon's model, not Caesar and still less Alexander. When he was still Bonaparte and, having read too much Plutarch, landed in Egypt, he was able for a moment to imagine himself Alexander; but it was only one campaign and only a dream. The Macedonian, wholly and solely a conqueror, never retraced his steps.

On the other hand the similarity between Charlemagne and Napoleon is astonishing. It is more than a resemblance; one might almost speak of a reincarnation, as if Charlemagne's soul, having wandered the earth for a thousand years, had at last found a lodging in the body of the child at Ajaccio.

Though there were a thousand years between them, those two conquerors pursued the same routes with their armies, performed the same deeds with the same consequences, governed, ruined and bled Europe in the same way. Both acquired their first fame in Italy by lightning campaigns, and continued their careers with wars in Germany; both built large fleets and reviewed them at Boulogne, but, restrained by other exigencies, gave up their intention of crossing to England; both failed in disastrous campaigns in Spain, where Joseph Bonaparte's demand for reinforcements echoes the appeal of Roland's horn; both, in the end, attacked the Slavs — the first, it must be allowed, with more success than the second. But Russia was neither a nation nor a state in Charlemagne's time.

Both Charlemagne and Napoleon had a taste for legislation and regulation. Europe lived for a long while under Charlemagne's Capitularies, which were continuously revised and altered, much as France still lives under the Napoleonic Code.

The first 'king of Rome' was not l'Aiglon, but young Pépin, Charlemagne's son, whom Charlemagne had baptised and at the same time crowned king of Italy on Easter Day 781. And this Pépin no more inherited the imperial throne than did Napoleon's son; he died before his father.

If Napoleon went one better than his predecessor when he snatched the crown from the pope's hands and placed it on his own head, he also surpassed him by marrying an imperial princess — the Austrian dynasty had the same mythical prestige for him as had the Byzantine dynasty for Charlemagne. On the other hand, he was less fortunate than Charlemagne in that he saw his empire fall to pieces during his own lifetime.

Charlemagne compelled all his subjects over the age of twelve to swear loyalty to his person before witnesses and on a reliquary. Those who refused were immediately imprisoned; and thereby the right of expressing opposition was somewhat limited. Napoleon demanded the oath only from his officials.

Among the benefactions humanity owes to Charlemagne Prussia must take first place; it was born of one of the great military provinces, or marches, which he had founded to protect the eastern frontiers of his realm. Populated by soldiers, administered by the sternest officers and most experienced generals, a scene of constant warfare, the Prussian march, on becoming a nation, remained faithful to its first vocation. When, in 1806, Napoleon signed the act giving birth to the German Confederation, the matrix of the German Empire, he revived, with consequences that we all know, Charlemagne's work, which the centuries with pain and bloodshed had reduced and nearly effaced. Of all Napoleon's deeds this was surely the most inauspicious.

The Carolingian Empire was a tyranny which bound disparate peoples together. When that empire was dismembered every pernicious aspect of nationalism was inevitably born. They were reborn with enhanced violence, and even narrower and more jealous rivalries, immediately after Napoleon's collapse.

Both Charlemagne and Napoleon favoured the establishment of a new governing class based on the sword, the altar and wealth. To a great extent, the bourgeoisie of the nineteenth century owed their power over national resources and the machinery of authority to Napoleon. This caused them, whether secretly or openly, to view him with a fond nostalgia.

The work of social stratification undertaken by Charlemagne had even more important and lasting results. He gave feudalism, of which the characteristics were still fluid, its final structure.

And what of Paris at this time? Paris was administered by a count — the one in Charlemagne's period was called Étienne — and its only importance was to be the seat of a *missatica*, that is to say a sort of super-préfecture whose jurisdiction, exercised by two *missi dominici*, one a layman, the other a cleric, extended over the neighbouring counties of Mulcien, Melun, Provins, Étampes, Chartres and Poissy. It would appear that Count Étienne had accumulated the functions of prefect and super-prefect.

But Paris is not even mentioned in Charlemagne's will, among the twenty-one 'metropolises' who received legacies. Rome, Milan, Cologne, Mainz, Salzburg, Bordeaux, Bourges, Besançon, Arles and Rouen all received gifts of gold and silver; Sens is on the list, which suggests that the roll of beneficiaries had been inspired by the archbishops. Paris did not inherit so much as a chalice, which makes it the more strange that the city saw fit to erect a statue to Charlemagne in front of Notre-Dame and one which does not even resemble the man it is supposed to represent.

Though it had ceased to be the seat of power, Paris remained a capital city in financial and commercial terms. It was called 'the market of the nations', and the great annual fair at Saint-Denis, instituted by Dagobert and encouraged by Childebert and Pépin the Short, lasted a whole month 'to allow merchants from Spain, Provence, Lombardy and other regions to attend'.

Apart from the sounds of commerce, and the ringing of coin from the mint which the emperor had authorised, there was silence on the banks of the Seine, a sort of historical torpor. The awakening was to be bloody.

Transporting with him, from Thionville to Worms, from Salestadt to Frankfurt, from Nijmegen to Mainz, from Aix-la-Chapelle to Rome, the errant capital of an impossible empire, Charlemagne was able to believe at his death that he had really constructed that *imperium christianorum* of which he dreamed, at once military and hierarchic, in which each inhabitant, no matter to what race he belonged, was uniformly subject to the same faith and the same law. The edifice collapsed immediately after his death; but the fragments of his dream have fought among each other from that day to this.

Vigorous nations, like living organisms, seem to secrete their own anti-toxins. Installed by Charlemagne to serve the Empire, the counts of Paris were to save France.

4 EUDES'S RESISTANCE

Scarcely had Charlemagne been buried at Aix-la-Chapelle than a multitude of long, black sea-dragons with shields for scales, each with thirty pairs of oars, half wings, half fins, came flying over the waves out of the Northern mists, like a chastisement or a nightmare.

Louis the Pious, abandoning the title of King of the Franks to retain only that of Emperor, was removed by his own sons, shut up in a monastery and then suddenly restored to the throne. His heirs, Charles, Louis and Lothair, disputing over the succession, fought among themselves killing sixty thousand men (the War of the Three Brothers), formed precarious alliances which they proclaimed before their troops (the Strasbourg Oath) sometimes in the Romance, sometimes in the Teutonic language, and finally concluded a partition (the Treaty of Verdun) which confirmed the division of the Empire. Aquitaine rebelled once again, and Brittany, roused by a former *missus* who donned the royal crown, declared itself independent, while the Saracens again moved northwards from the toe of Italy. The whole of Europe was sunk in appalling anarchy, and the Norsemen, who had appeared off the Channel coast at the turn of the century, carried their depredations even deeper into French territory year after year.

The Norse invasions, that extraordinary phenomenon of warlike migration by the Scandinavians during the ninth century, which was without precedent among these peoples and was never to be repeated, split into three main branches according to the different regions from which they set out.

The Norsemen from Sweden, or Varangians, operated in the Baltic and infiltrated into the east of the European continent. Within one generation, transporting their ships from river to river, they reached Kiev and made it their capital. In the next generation they reached the Black Sea; they attacked Constantinople in 860 and very nearly took it. Those men really did change the world, for it was under their sway and around their chiefs—the dynasty of Rurik—that the Russian nation took shape.

The Norsemen from Norway preferred to make their incursions into Scotland and Ireland.

The Danes, for their part, first scoured Belgium and then the shores of the Channel. They were pirates, wonderfully disciplined, organised and commanded, engaged on a great adventure of conquest. They rounded Finistère in 819, and in the next year passed the estuary of the Loire. From 833, taking advantage of the weakening of the imperial power, they mounted each year more numerous, audacious and terrifying expeditions.

In 841 they sacked and burnt Rouen. All the rich abbeys in the neighbourhood suffered the same fate or, like that of Saint-Wandrille, were held to ransom for great quantities of gold. Having a fondness for precious metals and corn, the Norsemen systematically attacked the religious establishments which they knew to be overflowing with these forms of wealth. The monks were either slaughtered or taken into captivity to labour as serfs. In 843 it was the turn of Nantes to be ravaged; the bishop was killed on the steps of the altar, and the prisoners were embarked in herds. The Norsemen, having moderately plundered the north of Aquitaine and reached the point where the Arabs had halted two centuries before, spent the winter in the mild climate of the Ile de Ré.

The anxious and much-tried bishops besought Charlemagne's grandsons, who were then in the brief honeymoon of amity after Verdun, to form a league against the Norse menace; but the Three Brothers were celebrating their 'Régime of Concord' and preferred to feast each other, or use their fighting men to make their own subjects acknowledge their rule.

As a result, at Easter 845, one hundred and twenty Danish ships attacked Paris. The people fled into the country; the city was sacked, and when the ships left they were down to the gunwales under the weight of booty. Among much else, the Norsemen carried away the splendid bronze roof of Saint-Germain-le-Doré.

Charles the Bald, King of *Francia Occidentalis*, was busy that year fighting the revolutionaries of Brittany and Aquitaine, both of whom defeated him. This was the Norsemen's opportunity. They extended their forays throughout the region, sailing up the Vilaine as far as it was navigable, up the Loire to Tours, and up the Garonne as far as Toulouse. Angers, Saintes and Nantes were again visited by them; while Bordeaux was burnt in 848. Four years later, the Viking Godfried, leading an expedition from the valley of the Scheldt to the Seine, set up his camp at Jeufosse, near Bonnières.

Charles the Bald wished to march against him; but his barons refused to fight and obliged him, somewhat shamefully, to parley.

Paris received another visitation at Christmas 856, and several churches lost their roofs. The Norsemen were now everywhere. Having passed the Straits of Gibraltar, they landed in the Camargue, sailed up the Rhône and appeared at Valence; they even went into Italy and took Pisa. And in 861, for the third time, a Norse expedition devastated Paris.

Pillaged and left defenceless three times in fifteen years, the people of Paris knew that they could expect nothing from their sovereign; they placed their hopes rather in Robert the Strong, former Count of Toulouse, then *missus* of Anjou and Maine, who had been given command of the whole duchy lying between the Loire and the Seine and extending from the sea to the counties of Nevers and Auxerre which it included. Robert was both an administrator and a soldier, and was genuinely at war with the Norsemen. But he was killed in a battle on the Loire in 866.

Meanwhile, what was the sinister Charles the Bald doing, that incoherent and obstinate prince who had France in his charge, who ceaselessly betrayed or was betrayed, and whose fortunes, constantly reversed, led him from the depths to the heights? Helpless to prevent the plunder and remedy the famine in his own realm, incapable of making himself obeyed or showing himself to be truly a king, he engaged his armies against those of his brother, Louis, and claimed the Lotharingian succession. He also aspired to the kingdom of Italy, put out the eyes of his son whom he suspected of plotting against him, and finally secured the imperial crown which had certainly blinded the Carolingians with its brilliance.

The people of Paris had watched from afar as Charles the Bald, having at last won a victory at Angers, neglected to exploit his success in his eagerness to claim the vacant empire; and then they had seen him ignore a new Norse landing at the mouth of the Seine while he pursued the Rhenish heritage and got himself beaten in the process.

Since they now trusted no one but themselves and their count, Eudes, the son of Robert the Strong, the people of Paris rebuilt the Roman walls round the Cité, fortified them and, to defend the approaches of the two bridges, built two small wooden castles, known as 'châtelets', in which permanent guards were mounted.

In the districts on the two banks there were more ruins than rebuilding. There was little incentive to build or indeed even to repair. On the other hand, the price of land in the Cité rose and the houses grew taller. As in the time of Attila, the market of the nations shrank back into the twenty-five acres of the original island.

At first these defensive measures seemed unnecesary. For several years the Norsemen seemed to have forgotten the Seine basin. They preferred their settlement in England, where King Alfred had ultimately ceded them a part of his territory, and to continue pillaging Provence, where an independent Kingdom of Arles had come into existence to combat them.

But in 880 part of the Norse army in England sailed down the Thames under a commander called Siegfried. Their first campaign took them up the Scheldt to Ghent. The next year they were at Cambrai and Amiens. A battle in which they suffered severe losses caused them to fall back on Lorraine. In 882 they returned, making this time for Rheims, from which the body of Saint Remi was hastily removed. In the summer of 885, Siegfried arrived before Rouen by water, took it, and continued up the Seine.

All the suburbs of Paris were evacuated and the population crowded on to the island, to which the treasures of the monasteries and the relics of the saints, as well as private fortunes, were removed. On 26 November, Siegfried, having been joined by another party of Norse from the Loire, reached the bridges of Paris with seven hundred sail, seven hundred dragon-headed prows. According to contemporaries, this fleet covered two leagues of the river.

Siegfried did not ask for the surrender of the city; all he wanted, he said, was that the people of Paris should destroy their Great Bridge to give passage to his ships. But the Parisians knew what a Norseman's word was worth, particularly when it was backed by thirty thousand iron-helmeted warriors with fierce faces and huge, rapacious hands.

For the first time a western city, without royal or imperial support, instead of surrendering, paying ransom or fleeing, said no to the Norsemen. Count Eudes, Bishop Gozlin and the population made the decision by common consent.

The siege of Paris lasted ten months. Entrenched on the right bank, around Saint-Germain-l'Auxerrois, the Norsemen set about building rams and engines of war. They launched their first assault on the Great Bridge on 31 January 886, and renewed it on 1 and 2 February. Bombardments with stone balls and flaming darts, fires which set the Châtelet, the wooden towers and the houses of the island alight, clouds of arrows flying over the arms of the Seine. To the scourge of war were added natural calamities. On 6 February—a date that was often dramatic for Paris, it would seem—a flood carried away the Little Bridge, which joined the Cité to the left bank, and allowed the enemy to take one of the two Châtelets. The river rose dangerously, making it easier for the besiegers to approach the ramparts. Men fought standing in water. Then famine broke out.

But Siegfried's seven hundred ships were still held downstream. The crown having passed from a bald man to a stutterer and then to a fat man, it was to the Emperor Charles the Fat, in Italy, that Count Eudes sent messengers, who slipped out of Paris at night, swimming, to ask for help and provisions.

The Emperor sent two weak expeditions. The first, under the command of Duke Henry of Saxe, contented itself with relieving the blockade and supplying the city; but it abstained from giving battle. The second was cut to pieces under the eyes of the besieged.

Bishop Gozlin died in April. Count Eudes continued to repel attacks, mounting the walls himself and attempting heroic sorties by the only bridge. Then, one night, he broke out of the city and galloped off to Germany, to remonstrate with Charles the Fat and persuade him to intervene in person.

Charles the Fat set out unwillingly, with so huge an army that when it came streaming down the heights of Montmartre the Norsemen in panic transferred their camp to the left bank. But although Charles the Fat liked power, he feared risk. Moreover, he was an epileptic. Rather than fight a battle in which he would have had a numerical advantage of four to one he chose to negotiate with Siegfried, guaranteeing him a free passage both ways so that he might go into Burgundy and pillage it undisturbed. He considered this an astute move, believing that he was making use of the Norse to punish Burgundy for its tendency to independence, and also checking the expansion of the new Kingdom of Arles, which now stretched from the Alps to the Cévennes and from the Jura to the Mediterranean.

The people of Paris were not impressed by this subtlety. To them it seemed that the Emperor was merely making the Norsemen a present of what they had been denied for the past ten months, the destruction of the Great Bridge. In addition, the Emperor had promised Siegfried seven hundred livres of silver when he left, as a farewell gift.

Count Eudes, in the name of Paris, refused to acknowledge the bargain which was not an act of cowardly betrayal.

The Emperor shrugged his fat shoulders, and the Norsemen, who had had enough, did what they might have done long before: they man-handled their seven hundred dragon-ships on to the river-bank and dragged them through the fields on rollers to refloat them a league upstream. It may be confidently asserted that this was the only battle-fleet which, on passage from the present site of the Pont d'Iéna to that of the Pont d'Austerlitz, ever crossed the Champ de Mars, the plain of Grenelle and the fields of Saint-Germain-des-Prés. The Norsemen had to repeat the process on their return, after subjecting unhappy Burgundy to the worst winter it had ever known.

The rest of the country was as much impressed by the resistance of Count Eudes as it was sickened by the Emperor's weakness. When, eighteen months later, Charles the Fat, having been deposed by the Diet of Triburg, died without issue, though not without pretenders to the succession, 'the kingdoms which had been subject to his dominion', wrote a chronicler, 'broke apart, and each tried to create a king drawn from its own entrails'.

When the bishops, counts and barons of *Francia Occidentalis* assembled they refused to hand over the crown to a Germanic prince, and in February 888, at Compiègne, they elected as their king Count Eudes of Paris.

Preceding his great-nephew, Hugues Capet, by a century, Eudes was the first king who may really be called a 'King of France'.

5 OTTO'S HALLELUJAH

The hundred years between the election of Eudes and that of the first Capet was a confused period during which Charlemagne's empire finally disintegrated. The kingdom of Germany was split into regional duchies. All over Europe independent kingdoms sprang up, some of which lasted only as long as their founders, while others were to create territorial or dynastic problems for centuries to come. The imperial sceptre passed from the hands of the Carolingians into those of varied dukes, but it was no more than an empty symbol until Otto I of Saxony created the German Holy Empire, an attempt to resurrect both the empire of the Caesars and that of Charlemagne.

Taking advantage of the widespread disorder, the Norsemen renewed their aggression; the Saracens enjoyed easy victories throughout the Mediterranean basin, and particularly in anarchic Italy; while the Hungarians, as if some virtue inherited from Attila had suddenly awakened in their veins, developed a fever for invasion which led them to cut their way with the greatest savagery as far as the plateaux of Champagne. Nor were the Hungarians, Saracens and the Norse alone in their ravages. Independent freebooters led no less redoubtable bands.

Owing to the impotence of the State, and indeed often its non-existence, the *fief*—a term of Gothic root of which the original meaning was 'herd'—appeared to be the only territorial, administrative, juridical and political notion which was both real and permanent; and the great feudal lords became the true kings. There are times when the people can turn for help only to the authors of the ills that beset them, and the dawning of the feudal system was one of these. Vassalage was a safeguard, a hope, and presently an honour. The highest ambition a freeman could possess was to join the 'herd' and enter into dependence. Only thus could he obtain protection and, with a little luck, a crumb of power. The Church took part in creating this system; diocese and county were often the same, and there were count-bishops among the most important feudal lords.

For a hundred years the crown of France, like a ball tossed from player to player, passed back and forth in a series of lobs between the Carolingian dynasty, which was approaching its end, and the rising house of Robert, later to be called that of Capet. It was a contest between two teams, the German princes and the counts of Paris.

The first challenge came five years after the election of Eudes. The son of Louis the Stammerer, Charles III, got himself elected and crowned by a party of nobles at Rheims. There were now two kings of France, two holders of the title, and of course they fought.

The elected sovereign of Germany at this period was Arnulf. He was a natural grandson of Louis the Germanic. Having successively recognised both Eudes and Charles as King of France, he played the part of arbitrator between them. The advantage remained temporarily with Charles, since Eudes died childless and designated Charles as his successor in order to restore peace. Eudes's brother, Robert, who was to become the representative of French hopes, accepted this and contented himself, or feigned to do so, with holding the counties of Paris, Tours, Blois and Angers, as the leading vassal of Charles III, named the Simple.

Why Simple? The nickname was wholly undeserved and is one of history's deceits. It would have been enough for a single chronicler, gratifying some personal spite, to apply to Charles III some such epithet as *parvus, minor, stultus* or *insipiens* for him to remain so branded down the centuries. In fact, this prince was very far from simple; he was one of the most intelligent of all the Carolingians. Following the

English example, he bought off the Norsemen by giving them in 911, under the Treaty of Saint-Clair-sur-Epte, the duchy which they were already occupying *de facto*, and which took the name of Normandy. The new duke, Rollo, having been converted with his followers to the official religion, became a great vassal of the king, and brought order to the territories which he had been looting only the year before. The feudal system had found its justification.

But at the same time Charles III annexed the kingdoms of Lorraine — the ancient Lotharingia or what remained of it — and assumed its crown; and this aggrandisement was fatal to him. Reigning over two kingdoms, he antagonised both his neighbours, the kings of Germany who coveted the same territories, and the French feudal lords who were exasperated at seeing the court move to the east and great offices pass to Lorrainers.

The second challenge came in 922, when Count Robert rebelled and an assembly deposed Charles and placed Robert on the throne. France again had two kings, and once again they fought. The battle took place in the neighbourhood of Soissons. Robert, who had only reigned for a year, was killed; but his army, led by his son Hugues, then nineteen years old and later to be called Hugues the Great, was victorious.

However, the French lords did not give the crown to Hugues, doubtless thinking him too young; they preferred his brother-in-law, Raoul, Duke of Burgundy, who was immediately proclaimed and crowned at Soissons. The ball was now passed across the field, as it were. So France had a king called Raoul who is never mentioned, and who was the only representative of the Burgundian line. It began and ended with him.

Charles III fell through treachery into the hands of Raoul and died after spending six years in various prisons. His wife, Queen Ogive, fled to England to her father Edward the Elder, taking with her a little Louis aged only two years.

After a difficult reign of thirteen years, principally notable for Hungarian invasions, Raoul died suddenly in 936, leaving no direct heir.

The third challenge came from the action of Hugues the Great. Although everything seemed to point to his election to the throne, his fear of family opposition, amid the general uncertainty, caused him to make a show of offering the crown to the Carolingians, who by then were virtually out of the running, and he brought the son of Charles the Simple and Queen Ogive out of exile. But he was being too clever. Louis, called 'the Englishman', or more often 'from Over the Sea', was crowned at Laon. Hugues had thought he could control this boy of fifteen and rule in his name. His disappointment was rapid and bitter.

The renewed rivalry between vassal and lord filled the whole reign, and once again there was an appeal to German arbitration. The reader may find the affair complex and tedious; it was infinitely more so for contemporaries.

This time the arbitrator was the Saxon Otto, the founder of the Holy Roman Empire, a man of great size. He first pronounced in favour of the vassal and, to support him, appeared with an army before Paris. In the event Louis from Over the Sea retained the crown but all the real power passed into the hands of Hugues the Great, for whom a new duchy was created round the county of Paris, the duchy of France, no longer a temporary military command, but a great hereditary fief. Shortly afterwards, Hugues received the duchy of Burgundy.

The king was now so weak that he was captured in an ambush laid for him by the inhabitants of Rouen. They handed him over to Hugues who immured him in a dungeon. However, Louis had by now married a sister of Otto and thus dealt himself a trump card. The German arbitrator reappeared, this time to favour the lord. Otto invaded France for the second time, took Rheims and paraded his troops up and down before Paris before leading them on to Rouen. It was a simple matter of showing the flag; but these military expeditions were hard on the local population. The heavy tread of boots and horseshoes along the banks of the Seine remained a sinister memory to Parisian ears.

Hugues was excommunicated. Since Pépin's coronation kings had been able to obtain such sanctions from their bishops. But Hugues also had bishops – so eventually duke and king were reconciled from mutual necessity. The Hungarians were back again threatening the neighbourhood of Rheims and Laon.

Louis IV from Over the Sea died at the age of thirty-three in a hunting accident. The crown then passed without hindrance to his son Lothair. The redoubtable shadow of Otto, the new Charlemagne, lay across the election. Hugues the Great, although his claim was powerful, did not put forward his candidature but sold his vote for the grant of the duchy of Aquitaine, and became regent, governing on behalf of the new king, who was only thirteen.

The duchies of France, Burgundy and Aquitaine were now all united in one hand; France was beginning to emerge from infancy and show an adult face. Hugues's greatness resides in having helped to mould this face.

As Lothair succeeded Louis from Over the Sea, so was Hugues the Great succeeded in his possessions and charge of the duchy of France by his son Hugues, who was called Capet.

What was the origin of this nickname which was to serve through the centuries as the surname of the French dynasty? Was it the word 'chapeau'? No it was more likely the word 'chape', the *cappa*. But what sort of *cappa*? The mediaevalists are not in agreement. Some maintain that it was the cope, the Church vestment, arguing that the Dukes of France were Abbots of Saint-Martin of Tours and wore the cope: others maintain that it was a short cloak which Hugues liked wearing. But again, which Hugues? The chroniclers of the eleventh century give the nickname to Hugues the Great, those of the twelfth to his son. Sometimes the origins of kings' names can be as obscure as those of the names of the most obscure citizens.

As long as the Emperor Otto I lived, which he continued to do for nearly twenty years, duke and king appear to have been in reasonable accord. But at the terrible Saxon's death, upon which his son Otto II became emperor, the hereditary disease of the Carolingians — the lure of the east — reappeared in Lothair, who assembled an army and made a lightning march on Aix-la-Chapelle. Hugues Capet made no attempt to prevent him, indeed even supported him discreetly with a few detachments, but without really becoming involved.

Poor Lothair! Poor scion of Charlemagne's stock, who believed himself triumphant when he entered the ancient palace of his ancestor, from which Otto II narrowly escaped. What dreams must have filled his mind! He had the bronze eagle with outspread wings, which decorated the roof, turned towards Germany like a threat, yet his glory came to an end with this one exploit. After three days, he had to retreat for lack of food, and his departing soldiers looted the palace.

As a reprisal, Otto II invaded France in pursuit of Lothair. He took Laon, and ravaged Champagne and the Soissonnais. He reached Paris, but here Hugues Capet, who had prudently retained most of his forces, barred the river crossing, while Lothair fled to Etampes to raise an army.

Throughout the month of November 978, Otto II camped on the heights of Montmartre, near the old church which still bore the Roman columns from the temple of Mercury embedded in its façade. The imperial troops laid waste to the neighbourhood and burned the northern suburbs; nevertheless the duke in his short cloak continued to fight for his capital, preventing access to the bridge, and harassing and containing the enemy.

Otto remained on his hill like a large insect buzzing against a window-pane; and finally, with winter approaching, and a counter-offensive imminent, he decided to give up. On the morning of 30 November, the day of his departure, he assembled his priests and ordered them to chant a great Hallelujah which was taken up by the whole army, to the amazement of the Parisians on their island. Sixty thousand men sang; their voices filled the sky from Montmartre, and the earth trembled, so it is said. The reason for this paean of rejoicing, sung by an emperor and his troops at the moment of retreat, will never be known.

It was rather for the Parisians to shout 'Hallelujah!' More than eight centuries were to elapse before another German army appeared at their gates.

Moreover the long dynastic uncertainty was soon to be ended. Eudes had saved Paris from the Norse; Hugues the Great had created the national duchy centred upon Paris; and Hugues Capet had now saved Paris from the Germans. His house, which had already produced three kings, was truly illustrious. The competition for the throne was entering its last phase. The first error of the rival house gave victory to the dynasty of Paris.

As we approach the year 1000 and realise that half the history of the capital has been covered, as we count the centuries and see that there are as many between Caesar and Hugues Capet as there were between Hugues Capet and ourselves, we may well wonder how the time passed so quickly. How did the years slip away, leaving so little trace?

But there were the Carolingians, and two centuries are virtually missing. The reigns that filled them resemble the bad days in all our lives, frittered away in failure and ill-conceived beginnings, which leave behind them neither achievement nor true memories, but only regrets.

Chapter 4

The Capital of the Capets

I ADALBÉRON'S ASSEMBLY

THOUGH IT did not take place in Paris, Hugues Capet's election directly concerned the city. It restored Paris to the position of capital, which it had not in fact enjoyed since the death of Dagobert. Let us take a look at how this election came about.

When the Emperor Otto II was in full retreat King Lothair intercepted him, not in order to crush him but to conclude an alliance with him against the Duke of France. On Lothair's part, this was carrying ingratitude rather far, since Hugues had just saved him; and when, shortly afterwards, Otto died suddenly in Rome, and rivalries broke out in the Empire between the Saxons and the Bavarians, Lothair, in the same high-minded fashion, promptly abandoned his previous allies, the Saxon party, and joined Henry of Bavaria in snatching Lorraine from Otto's successor, who was then a child of three.

Betrayal may sometimes serve the exigencies of high policy; but it is not in itself an adequate system of government, nor does any man become a great monarch solely by treachery.

The Archbishop of Rheims at that time happened to be a Lorrainer called Adalbéron, who owed his career to the Ottos and had remained deeply attached to them. Lothair, on taking Verdun, seized the whole Adalbéron family and imprisoned them.

But coercion is no more certain a guarantee of victory than betrayal, and what had succeeded with Charlemagne was not necessarily to succeed with Lothair. The Archbishop of Rheims was an extremely important person and his position in the feudal hierarchy was that of a duke or count. Moreover, Adalbéron, a man of learning and lively intelligence, had become famous throughout Christendom for the school he had founded near his cathedral, where he had assembled the most erudite faculty. Adalbéron's word carried authority and his pupils spread his influence far and wide. Lothair was attacking a formidable opponent.

Adalbéron negotiated secretly with Hugues Capet, and letters began to circulate, strangely recalling Pope Zacharius's remarks about Pépin the Short: 'The King of France, Lothair, is head only in name; Hugues is not so in name, but he is so in fact...'

Lothair got wind of the plot and summoned the Archbishop to appear before an ecclesiastical assembly at Compiègne, but when the assembly was brought together Hugues Capet appeared with his forces and dispersed it. This was in May 985.

Lothair pretended to lose interest in the matter and soon afterwards did so in fact, for he died, wholly unregretted. This was in March 986.

The succession was already settled, since Lothair had taken the precaution, during his lifetime, of having his son, Louis V, crowned as co-regent. Louis V, therefore, continued his father's government with unbroken continuity and laid seige to Rheims. Adalbéron declared that there was no reason why the town should suffer for unproven accusations made against its prelate. He offered to go in person to justify himself before any assembly or tribunal that might be appointed. The whole of France was stirred; Louis V was compelled to yield to public opinion; he raised the siege and again summoned an assembly at Compiègne. This brings us to May 987.

On the very day the assembly began its deliberation, Louis V was killed in a hunting accident. Either providence, in the form of a tree or a boar's tusk, declared most opportunely for Capet and Adalbéron, or else they gave destiny a hand. The Carolingians had always enjoyed matching themselves against wild beasts, Pépin the Short had even gone into the arena against them; Charlemagne had been wounded attacking a wild boar with a spear, while Louis from Over the Sea had died of his passion for hunting. It was the most natural and most likely way for any member of this family to die.

Hugues Capet at once assumed presidency of the assembly, and Adalbéron, whose position as the accused was rapidly forgotten, opened and closed the meeting with a single speech in which he persuaded all those present to swear to take no steps for the election of a new king until the great nobles of the kingdom could meet in plenary session at Senlis. Here, before the end of the month, the electoral campaign was briskly conducted. The Carolingian faction could advance only one name, that of Charles of Lorraine, the uncle of Louis V, and he had little support among the French Lords.

Adalbéron, completely controlled the assembly at Senlis. His speech, which opened the way to the Capet monarchy, has been preserved. He was an intellectual with a gift of oratory, and with him a new epoch and a new style began.

Playing on national sentiment, he drew a dark portrait of the Carolingian pretender, a prince, he declared, 'not guided by honour but weakened by sloth, who has so lost his wits that he has no shame in serving a foreign king'. Hugues, on the other hand, was worthy 'by his actions, his nobility, and his troops'... 'The throne', Adalbéron went on, 'is not to be taken by hereditary right, and we must put at the head of the kingdom a man who is distinguished not only for his physical nobility, but also for his qualities of mind, a man whom honour recommends and magnanimity supports.'

Hugues Capet was elected on 1 January 987. Paris, which had seen a duke set out for Senlis, saw a king return.

A month later the new sovereign was solemnly crowned by the archbishop in Rheims Cathedral. Hugues owed Adalbéron nothing less. Thereafter, Rheims was to be the place of coronation, not because of Saint Remi or the baptism of Clovis, but in the tradition of the crowning of Hugues Capet.

2 ROBERT'S PALACE

The nine years of Hugues Capet's reign were not easy ones.

'Who made you a count?'

'Who made you a King?'

This exchange between Hugues and Aldebert of Perigord, although it may be the invention of a later chronicler, sums up the problems of government in early days of the dynasty. It was in this dramatic fashion that the feudal lords addressed the sovereign who owed his crown to their votes.

Nor is it surprising: the worst difficulties of any new régime are likely to come from the men who helped to establish it, who seldom believe that they are heard or favoured according to their deserts.

In 996 Hugues Capet died and the crown passed to his son Robert II.

France has had no Shakespeare, or she might better understand the strange character and destiny of the second Capet. History takes note of a good many princes who deserved to be called 'the pious', and of an equal number who were excommunicated; but this is the only case of a monarch who was both.

He had a physical peculiarity which the people of Paris remarked as he rode through the streets: his feet were so supple that his big toe almost met his heel round the stirrup. He was no less singular in character.

Theologian, musician and mystic, he could sing the office better than a priest, and it is said that he composed several psalms. He commissioned a magnificent gold reliquary to receive the oaths of allegiance of his lords, but kept it empty rather than risk the profanation of the holy relics by an act of perjury. So much for his opinion of his vassals' good faith! He also had a silver reliquary containing nothing but a thrush's egg which he reserved for the oaths of peasants and people of low degree.

Robert II gave generously to charity and, on feast days, allowed the poor to come to his table so that he might distribute presents to them. But his behaviour was sometimes unexpected. When a blind man approached him while he was washing his hands before an Easter feast, he threw the basin of water in his face. The blind man's eyelids must have been stuck together with mucus, for he instantly recovered his sight. The word went round that the king had performed a miracle and thereafter he was pursued by the afflicted and the merely curious wherever he went.

The whimsicality which was at the root of Robert II's character also appeared in his political and private actions. The utopian who proposed a project for universal peace to the Emperor Henry II of Germany, and supported the Truce of God which followed the Council of Elne, was also the precursor of the Inquisition. He had the notion of suppressing heresy and prided himself on having burned alive at Orléans fourteen persons 'from among the best priests and leading laymen of that town'.

Pious though he was, he repudiated his first wife, Rosala of Italy, in order to contract a love-match with his cousin, Berthe of Burgundy, the widow of the Count of Blois; and although a fanatical servant of the Church he by no means lost his keen sense of the royal prerogative, and sought to retain his right to appoint ecclesiastics of his own choice to the bishoprics of his realm. This was the cause of his conflict with Rome. The Pope, who tolerated far worse scandals in the chapters of abbeys and cathedrals, used their cousin-marriage as a pretext for excommunicating Robert the Pious and Queen Berthe, and the kingdom was placed under an interdict.

Legend has it that the king was then abandoned by his subjects, who fled him as if he had the plague. All his charities and psalm-singing, and even his miracle, went for nothing. A chronicler writes that he lived alone in his Palais de la Cité where 'there remained to him only two wretched servants who prepared his food, and even these looked with abhorrence on the vessels the king used for eating and drinking and threw the remains of his meal on the fire'.

A touching picture, and one which is embedded in childhood memories, together with the tale of the panic in the year 1000, when the people crowded into the churches expecting to see the roofs split open to the sounding trumpets of the Day of Judgement. As so often in the accounts of chroniclers, there is a grain of truth in the sackful of fable; but the year 1000 passed like any other and the heavens kept silence.

And the King of France remained king.

Robert resisted papal pressure for five years, but finally yielded. Dismissing the queen he loved, he married a Provençale, Constance of Arles, who was unrelated to him but had a most disagreeable character. She filled his days with tantrums and nagging, and peopled his court with plotters, thieves and debauchees from among the southern lords. Morality, as we see, had scored a victory.

Robert the Pious did much rebuilding. In addition to the reconstruction of the abbeys of Saint-German-des-Prés and Saint-Germain-l'Auxerrois, which had remained in ruins since the Norse invasions, Paris is indebted to him for the complete remodelling of the Palais de la Cité.

Perhaps he hoped in this way to efface the bad memory of his excommunication, or to restore his temporarily diminished authority by the majesty of his dwelling; or perhaps, more simply, the palace showed signs of wear. It had stood on Roman foundations for a thousand years, it had served the kings of the first race, but those of the second had despised it. The counts of Paris, later the dukes of France and finally the kings of France, had established their residence and their administration there, but in a period of warfare and insecurity they had maintained it only to the extent of their immediate needs. Robert intended to make his palace remarkable, a *palatium insigne*. The new Capet dynasty would remake Paris from the beginning.

Indeed, his palace *was* remarkable. Seventeen successive kings were to live in it from the year 1000 to the middle of the fifteenth century. Enlarged and altered many times, flanked with towers and new buildings, maltreated in some reigns and improved in others, it was embellished by Louis IX with the Sainte-Chapelle, by Philip the Fair with the Merchant's Gallery, and by Charles V with the clock-tower. When finally, at the end of the Hundred Years' War, Charles VII moved his court to the Louvre, he left in the Palais de la Cité one of the first of the King's functions, one of its major powers, the dispensation of Justice; and Justice is still housed there.

The great bell of the clock-tower, intended to ring only at the births and deaths of kings, was to ring out during the night of St Bartholomew, replying to the alarm call of Saint-Germain-l'Auxerrois; yet on one occasion the Parliament of Paris, representing the continuity of the State in that same palace, during the wars of religion, prohibited by a papal legate from occupying the king's vacant throne; and on more than one occasion Parliament in its legal fortress, was to oppose the king himself by refusing to ratify his decisions.

In the seventeenth century a large part of Philip the Fair's additions to the Palais de la Cité was destroyed by fire, including the great statues of the sovereigns and the famous Marble Table, and another fire in the eighteenth century necessitated further rebuilding. These renovations in contemporary modes, and the various restorations carried out in the nineteenth century, made the Palace what it is today, so that it now resembles a catalogue of French architectural styles.

Litigants still take their conflicts there, advocates unfold their arguments, and judges give judgment. Crime is prosecuted there, as it was before the first kings; and the court of Appeal sits more or less where St Louis's Chamber sat.

There are certainly more beautiful, more homogeneous and more harmonious buildings in the world, but there is none more moving, none in which the stones are so linked, faced and cemented with the destinies of men, none in which at every step so long a history is traversed. Yet the king who had built the palace complained during his last years, that he could obtain no justice for himself. His rebellious sons were pillaging and burning his lands, treating their father in the manner of feudal lords.

3 ANNE'S DISAPPOINTMENT

The tragedy of the new dynasty was the feudalism it inherited from the old.

Rarely was a ruling class so little civilised as that of the lords, great and small, shut away in their bleak, square fortresses who emerged from them only to see heads bowed and animals flee. Hunting, war, adultery, and rape if need be, were their sole occupations. Nor were the women any better than the men; they fought and hunted with ruthless audacity, to gratify brutish appetites, and the ladies of the manor in the year 1000 can have been little more attractive than the common men-at-arms. If by chance they developed a taste for the arts, it led them, as it did Aubrée d'Ivry, to decapitate their architect so that he might not repeat his achievements for the benefit of others.

Free men had almost vanished from the countryside. The lords compelled men to be serfs, and where a family had lived in serfdom for several generations it might find itself, owing to the system of divided inheritances, shared by several owners, the children separated like cattle. No society was more reactionary, for law was based entirely on custom. 'Our fathers had this right, this privilege, this licence...' That was the feudal code. A highway robbery committed by a lord at the entrance to his domain, a plundered traveller, a ransom extracted from a passer-by, could establish a precedent and thus become an accepted toll, a right passing from father to son. There were no laws but only habits which, more often than not, were merely the repetition of an abuse.

Even the Church, well endowed with lands and human livestock, gave its blessing to this order of things. One might suppose that the Gospel was no longer taught when a monk could write: 'All power comes from God, who by an admirable and sovereign dispensation has placed on the earth kings, dukes and other men charged with authority over the rest. These were established by God so that the lesser men, as is logical, should be subordinate to the greater. God himself has willed that among men some should be lords and others serfs.' An astonishing sentiment: but we may remind ourselves, we who are contemporary with the Third Reich, that men in our time have maintained the same principles for different ends.

Such was the administrative capacity of the lords of the manor that famine, or at least serious scarcity, occured on an average two years out of three. Uprising and rebellion were the serf's only resort. These revolts, which were later to be called *jacqueries*, date from around the year 1000. The first hymn to liberty, the first revolutionary song to be sung in France, was as follows:

> Nous sommes hommes comme ils sont,
> Tels membres avons comme ils ont,
> Et tout aussi grand corps avons,
> Et tout autant souffrir pouvons;
> Ne nous faut que coeur seulement.

> We are men such as they,
> We have limbs such as they,
> We have bodies as tall,
> We can suffer as much;
> We lack only the heart.

The Normans who sang it had their hands and feet cut off.

When Anne of Kiev arrived in Paris in about 1050, to marry King Henri I who had succeeded to Robert the Pious, she wrote despairing letters to her father Yaroslav the Great, sovereign of Russia. In these she complained that she had been sent to a barbarous country where the houses were gloomy, the churches ugly and the customs revolting. For though the Russian nation had existed for only two centuries, Kiev, a capital ruled by princes, considered itself the rival and almost the equal of Byzantium. It had copied Constantinople's sumptuous architecture, its arts, its pompous luxury, profusion of wealth and imposing ceremonial. Poor Princess Anne must have made her journey in the mist of illusion, believing that in the King of the Franks she was marrying Clovis and Charlemagne rolled into one, and that Paris was a western Byzantium. Her disappointment can be imagined when she found a bridegroom of nearly forty-five, prematurely exhausted by ceaseless expeditions, a boor who mumbled Latin when the only language she spoke perfectly was Greek, a king who trafficked shamelessly in ecclesiastical benefices and yet was never sure he would not have his pocket picked if he ventured more than three leagues from his palace.

And Henri I in concluding this first Franco-Russian alliance may have dreamed of impressing the vassals who were combined against him and demonstrating his royal importance at the other end of the world. Or perhaps it was simply that he could not fool anyone nearer home.

This fanciful King of Paris, who sent the bishops of Soissons and Meaux across the steppes to bring him home a wife, was the same who allowed himself to be trapped in Fécamp, who frittered away his reign in attempts to assert his authority over Sens and barely triumphed at Villeneuve-Saint-Georges. For this was the limit of his power, this his real kingdom. Never had so small a France received a queen from so far away.

Because a few drops of Byzantine blood were mingled with the Swedish blood of her ancestors, Anne of Kiev sincerely believed that she was descended from Philip of Macedon and Alexander the Great. This was why she called her eldest son Philip. Six kings of France owed it to a Russian princess that they bore this Greek Christian name.

Philip I occupied the throne for forty-eight years, during thirty-eight of which he held personal power. Had he been a great king, he would be remembered. But he had no memorable virtues, indeed no virtues at all; his character was a mass of petty vices. He was gluttonous, venal, cynical and probably cowardly, caring only for comfort and sensual satisfaction. He never kept his word. When he lacked money, he took the easiest way of procuring it, either plundering the treasure of Saint-Germain-des-Prés or leasing the royal army to the highest bidder among his vassals.

Excommunicated for a doubly adulterous marriage, he made no tragedy of it as his grandfather had done. He bore with equanimity all the anathemas flung at him by the Councils of Clermont, Tours, Poitiers and finally Paris which were assembled to condemn him. Ultimately he took an oath to separate from his wife, but continued to live with her as before.

Philip I did nothing of importance, although great things took place during his reign.

William, Duke of Normandy, embarked upon the conquest of England, and Philip was not displeased to see that turbulent vassal depart. He was less pleased when the conquering bastard reappeared in arms on the road to Paris. Luckily for Philip, the Conqueror was mortally wounded at the taking and sacking of Mantes, and the Norman campaign ended there.

Pope Urban II decreed the First Crusade, and Philip watched approvingly while Peter the Hermit led a horde of starving peasants, fanatics, beggars and adventurers across Germany, Hungary and Bulgaria. The People's Crusade, as it was called, which pillaged Europe as it passed, diminished in numbers through disease and exhaustion on its journey, and the survivors were annihilated at their first encounter with the Turks.

He approved still more of the 'regular' crusade, that of the nobles, which is estimated to have included a hundred thousand knights and a million men in all, and which by countless land and sea routes drained France of her ambitious feudal lords, who vanished into Asia Minor by way of Constantinople.

While the crusaders, despite their crushing losses, despite sun, thirst and plague, mass desertions and the bitter rivalries of their leaders, took Antioch after an eight months' siege and founded at Jerusalem a Latin kingdom for Godfrey de Bouillon, all that Philip I achieved was to hold Montfort l'Amaury, and take Septeuil and Houdan. His greatest ambitions took him no farther than Valois or Sologne; and his greatest concern was for the keep of Montlhéry, the lair of minor brigand lords, who cut the road between Paris and Orleans. Eventually, not long before his death, Philip succeeded in taking this fortress. It was his most brilliant success. 'Guard that tower well,' he said to his son Louis; 'it has made me old before my time. The perfidy and wickedness of those who lived in it have never given me a moment's peace.'

The peculiarity of a great institution is that it will work even with second-rate men. That the Capet monarchy was able to survive kings such as Henri and Philip I proves that it had a certain strength. There were lords who fought the monarchy and pillaged its possessions, but they no longer contested its right to rule.

4 LOUIS'S DOMAIN

Louis VI produced a marked change of style. Like all the Capets, he was obsessed with the importance of his capital city, guarding its approaches, controlling the roads leading to it, increasing the domain around it, and on the strength of this enforcing respect for Paris on the other duchies and great lordships of the kingdom. But he brought a new vigour to the task. Elected and crowned during his father's lifetime, as were all the first Capets, it was he who commanded the army during Philip's last years; the taking of Montlhéry was in fact his victory.

'An incomparable athlete and an eminent gladiator,' as the Abbé Suger was to write, Louis VI earned the nicknames of 'the Warrior' and 'the Alert', before he became 'the Fat'.

He certainly had exceptional physique, and perhaps the blood of the steppes came out in the second generation. A memorable trencherman, he became so fat that from the age of forty he had to be hoisted into the saddle; but he had a wild courage, and regardless of warnings would always ride into the thickest of the fight. He did so at Chevreuse, Neauphle, Corbel and other places which today are the Sunday resorts of Parisians.

The fat king was not content with cleaning up his own domain by force. He bought, traded, confiscated, burned or pulled down suspect strongholds, pitilessly chastised their piratical owners, enfranchised their serfs and by granting municipal charters to certain towns altered the balance of local power. Having put his own house in order, he could afford to do the same for others, these being great vassals, and the work took nearly a third of a century.

He crossed the Oise and restored the Duchy of Normandy to its original frontiers. He challenged King Henry I of England to a duel on a bridge across the Epte in the presence of both armies, but Henry refused. He swam across the Indre, at the head of his troops. He marched on Arras, Berry and Auvergne, everywhere proving himself a king and that the king, as Suger says, 'had a long arm'.

He married, rather late, an excellent and extremely ugly woman who bore him nine children to assure the future of his line. Paris, sure of its dynasty, a capital of real authority, gained a new strength. Wealth and intelligence once again took up their habitation on the left bank; the monks canalised the Bièvre; new lands were drained and former fields were built over. Villages were absorbed into the city and only their steeples showed where they once had been. Commerce and crafts revived and multiplied on the right bank, above all commerce in food. Along the Quai de Grève, later called the Quai de l'Hôtel de Ville, the port of Paris came into being, its various wharves separated by flour-mills—wharves for hay, grain, wood, wine, coal and salt. Round the Grand Châtelet, which Louis the Fat rebuilt in stone so that it was no longer a mere guard-house shaped like a tower but a real fortress, a whole district concerned with victualling grew up and the different trades gave to the streets their descriptive names—Rue de la Grande Boucherie, de la Pierre à Poisson, de la Tuerie, de l'Écorcherie, Rue Pied de Boeuf, Rue de la Poulaillerie, Rue de l'Araigné (this last, the Street of the Spider, being derived from the four-branched hooks on which the butchers hung their meat). Paris eight centuries later is still supplied with food from the same neighbourhood, for this is where the Halles have been built.

Under Louis VI, Paris was alert like its king, and ate like him. She sold, traded and grew rich. In the eyes of the provinces and other towns in the kingdom, apart from a few big cities in Provence and Languedoc, Paris had become a civilised centre whose inhabitants were more independent and responsible than those elsewhere. It was true that the city was the joint possession of the king and bishop, and that most of its people were subject to toll in kind or labour and did not *belong* to themselves. There was an urban serfdom just as there was a rural one. Nevertheless, the *haute bourgeoisie* consisted of free men, and the trades were already organised in guilds, the trades unions of the Middle Ages. And like the merchandise in the shops and the money on the money-changers' counters, ideas circulated more rapidly and in greater number in Paris. In business quarters, which must have resembled the *suks* of Islamic cities, buyers, sellers, carriers, cripples and beggars formed a continuous milling crowd.

We know that animals wandered freely about the streets, because this caused the death of an important member of the royal family. Louis the Fat's eldest son, Prince Philip, already elected and joint occupant of the throne, was killed when his horse shied at a herd of pigs in the neighbourhood of Saint-Gervais.

Louis VI then had his second son elected and crowned, a Louis who was nicknamed 'the Young' because he was only eleven. We cannot tell what France may have lost by the death of Prince Philip, but certainly she gained nothing from his younger brother. To prevent the course of history being further affected, pigs were no longer allowed to wander loose in the streets, unless they belonged to the monastery of Saint-Antoine and then they had to wear bells round their necks.

Louis VI's ultimate success was to reunite Aquitaine with the crown, and this he achieved without a battle. After centuries of exhausting conflict between the Duchy of Aquitaine and the Kingdom of France, a wise king with a son, and a wise duke with a daughter, decided to marry their children and their states. Duke Guillaume X on his deathbed placed the safe-keeping of his duchy in the hands of Louis VI, together with the guardianship of his sole heiress, Eleanor so that she might marry the heir to the throne. The marriage of Louis the Young and Eleanor took place in 1137. And while the nuptials were being celebrated in Bordeaux—they were the nuptials of all France, the nuptials of *Oïl* and *Oc*—the plump warrior in the Palais de la Cité, as if he felt his task was done, lay dying of chronic dysentery on a carpet over which he had had ashes spread in the form of a cross.

Louis VI could close his eyes in the assurance that he had fulfilled his kingly task. The frontiers of his power when he acquired it had extended no further than Montlhéry; now they reached to the Pyrenees.

5 THE SCHOOL OF ABÉLARD

It was also during the reign of Louis VI, that time of profusion, that a young man emerged who was to establish Paris as the capital of the intellectual world. He was a Breton from the neighbourhood of Nantes and his name was Abélard.

He has remained famous above all for his love for the beautiful Héloise and the disaster which put an end to it. His name was even turned by popular malice into the verb 'abélardiser', an honour he could well have done without, since it means 'to castrate'. This misfortune, and his love-letters which are partly apocryphal, have made us forget what he was really like.

There was never so precocious or so brilliant a philosopher. At an age when his contempories were still students he was already teaching. Wherever an illustrious teacher appeared, as at Corbeil or Melun, he would dispute with him, destroy his arguments, and rob him of his audience. Self-confident to the point of arrogance, handsome and aware of it, witty, mocking, conscious of his intellectual superiority and armed with a profound knowledge of Aristotle which gave him an assured advantage over his adversaries, the young man had everything he needed to make his elders hate him. On the other hand, he was infinitely attractive to the young.

He described the beginning of his career thus: 'I began to travel about the provinces, going wherever I heard that the study of this art [dialectics] was held in honour, and everywhere I disputed in true emulation of the peripatetics. I aspired to the government of the schools...'

Abélard was only twenty-three when, at the dawn of the twelfth century, he arrived in Paris: a Paris where no one dared oppose Guillaume de Champeaux, considered the leading rhetorician of the age, who taught at the episcopal school of Notre-Dame. But Abélard dared, and went even further; he opened his own school in the cloister of Sainte-Geneviève. Students crowded to the lessons, deserting Champeaux's. Before long this philosopher with a boy's face had three thousand youths and girls hanging on his lips and dogging his footsteps. He had all the talents; he was a poet, a musician and a singer. One of the girls fell in love with him, which is nothing unusual. It surprises us only because it happened so long ago, and perhaps because it shows that even in that remote century there were young ladies of good family sufficiently cultivated to sit at the feet of a fashionable master. Clearly there had been a great and rapid change since Carolingian times.

Héloise was surely not alone in dreaming of Abélard, but doubtless she had more charm, beauty and intelligence than her companions, for Abélard fell in love with her. Dialectic was not the only subject of their conversations, and soon, neither master nor pupil having bothered about marriage, the beautiful Héloise was pregnant. Abélard abducted her and took her to Brittany, where he married her secretly. And here she gave birth to a son.

Unfortunately for Abélard, Héloise was the niece of Canon Fulbert of the chapter of Notre-Dame. That his own niece should have been seduced by the upstart who had emptied the episcopal school of its audience was more than the Canon could bear. He hired some ruffians who one night abducted Abélard and forced him to undergo a savage operation, carried out by some bribed barber, which ensured that he would never repeat his offence.

Abélard went to nurse his wounds in the Abbey of Saint-Denis, and because of his mutilation resolved to renounce the world and enter the Church. He persuaded Héloise to do the same, and it was from the

Convent of Argenteuil that she wrote him those celebrated letters which makes it clear that the fire burning within her was not wholly sacred.

Abélard had been forced into chastity, but not into silence. He revealed the cause of his misfortune —this was perhaps a mistake —an account of the affair that was widely circulated; and he set out to teach again. Being now a monk, he gave his personal interpretation of theology, and this caused him to be arraigned before a council at Soissons, which condemned his books to be burnt and his person to be confined. Back in Saint-Denis he turned to history and proved, long before modern scholars, that Denys, Bishop of Athens, had not been the first Bishop of Paris. This scandalous assertion led to his being expelled from the royal abbey. He became a hermit, living in a hut of reeds and thatch near Nogent-sur-Seine. But solitude did not suit him. His disciples came to join by hundreds when he let them know where he was, and he wrote tenderly of how they 'abandoned cities and castles to live in a desert, quitting vast dwellings for little huts they built with their own hands, exchanging delicate foods for wild herbs and coarse bread, soft beds for stubble and moss, their tables for grassy banks...' Well, Abélard was a great writer. Moreover he knew it, for he was not given to modesty. 'My body remained in that place but my fame spread throughout the world and filled it with my voice... Thenceforth I considered myself the only philosopher on earth and saw no rival whom I need fear...'

But his career was not yet ended. After ten years spent in a monastery in Brittany, among debauched monks whom he vainly tried to reform, and in strife with neighbouring local lords who tried to poison him, Abélard returned to Paris. He was fifty-five; his authority now lay in a considerable body of written work, largely the fruit of his Breton exile: *Introductio ad Theologiam, Dialectica, De Intellectibus, De Generibus et Speciebus*, a book on ethics entitled *Scito te ipsum* and a *Sic et non* on the rational search for truth.

He based himself on Plato and Aristotle, on Virgil and Lucan; he was a Renaissance man three centuries before the Renaissance. His return to the capital provoked delirious enthusiasm. His former pupils were now mature men and women; but their children, with the same fervour, climbed the slopes of the Montagne-Sainte-Geneviève to listen to the universal master of whom they had heard so much. His courses were received with acclamation.

But he was not to end his life amid universal applause, for again the Church was roused. They sent their most powerful champion against him, Saint Bernard himself, the redoubtable Abbot of Clairvaux. Saint Bernard, the reformer of the Cistercian order and the preacher of the Second Crusade, was no philosopher but a pamphleteer in the service of God. 'We have in France a monk without a rule...a prelate without solicitude, an abbé without discipline, a tortuous adder creeping out of his hole, a new hydra who grows seven heads for every one cut off...' wrote Saint Bernard to the cardinals.

Abélard took up the challenge and demanded to be confronted with his adversary in council. Abélard against Saint Bernard: the fight between dialectic and dogma, reason and faith, pure intelligence and effective action... What a splendid duel it would have been, its sparks still lighting the Middle Ages for us! But it did not take place.

The Council assembled at Sens. At first, Bernard refused to appear before it, writing to the Archbishop that 'he was only a child, that his adversary had been inured to argument since his youth, and that moreover he thought it shameful to coerce the faith founded on truth itself with subtle human quibbles'. Being warned that if he did not come he would fail his own cause, Bernard finally showed himself; but he refused to dispute with Abélard. He merely quoted seventeen propositions extracted from Abélard's writings and declared them to be erroneous — in plain language, heretical.

Abélard refused to stay even to the end of the reading; he left, banging the doors of the Council, and shouting that he would appeal to the pope. He was condemned without being heard. Having sought refuge in the Abbey of Cluny, he ended his days, sick and unhappy, three years later in a priory of the order at Châlons.

But Abélard had sown seeds on the Montagne-Sainte-Geneviève which no Council could destroy. His method of teaching, followed by his disciples, continued to attract students from every country and to shape new teachers. His 'school' survived him so successfully that it still exists. It was the embryo of that institution which, less than seventy-five years after his death, received the official name of the University of Paris.

Chapter 5

The Work of Centuries

I SUGER'S BASILICA

'FOR YOUNG KINGS old ministers' — Such might have been the motto of the ensuing reign. The great man of Paris and of France in the time of Louis VII was not the king but the Abbé Suger.

Sickly in appearance and weak in health, but endowed with a clarity of mind, a memory and a fund of energy which were equally astonishing, Suger was the first of those great ministers, devoted to the public good, who, on the many occasions when the royal power was exercised by an inadequate sovereign, ruled from behind the throne. Advocate to Saint-Denis before he became its abbot, he had displayed such ability that Louis VI appointed him to his Council and charged him with the conduct of ecclesiastical affairs throughout the realm, an extremely important post since the Church was morally involved in all social legislation. Moreover, the Church was passing through a serious crisis, for this was the period of the anti-popes and also of the first 'reform', which sought to deal with the morals of the clergy and the reorganisation of the chapters. Suger had occasion to travel to Rome four times; he knew about everything and had a hand in everything.

Louis the Young inherited from his father not only a unified kingdom, a docile army and sound finances, but also this eminent servant of the state. Suger's policy was based on the concept of a central government designed to make not only individuals but cities, trades and institutions directly dependent upon the central power. Communal charters were widely granted by the king, who thereby gained a measure of urban control, while new towns were also created, including most of those called Villeneuve; and these became immediate dependencies of the king. Professional guilds were incorporated under the royal aegis in which the precise conditions of each trade were laid down.

In Paris, the first calling to receive legal recognition and submit to
regulation was the ancient company of the 'water merchants', descendants of the first boatmen of Lutetia. The mercers followed and
their conditions of establishment and business were defined in the year
of Louis VII's accession. The butchers, and thereafter the five trades
dealing with leather—cobblers, purse-makers, harness-makers, tanners
and dressers—were incorporated, the last having left its name to the
Quai de la Grande Mégisserie.

In thus 'royalising' as many sections of French life as possible, and
giving them jurical and administrative apparatus, Suger, a progressive,
wise and patient man, sought to combat the abuses inherent in the
confusion of feudalism. Louis VII would have done well to listen to
him when he tried to dissuade him from undertaking the Second
Crusade. Opposition to this venture was general, the king alone being
its progenitor. The great barons, who had borne the expenses of the
First Crusade, retained bitter memories of that disastrous affair. Even
the hot-headed Saint Bernard was opposed to a second crusade and
refused to advocate it in the absence of a direct command from Rome.

But Louis was stubborn, partly perhaps from a desire to acquire
personal glory and thereby eclipse the memory of his father, beside
whom he cut an insignificant figure. He may also have found it hard to
accept his Minister's too obvious superiority, and perhaps, too, he
wanted to reinstate himself in the eyes of his wife, Eleanor who was
showing signs of chilliness and boredom. But, after all, perhaps he
really did believe that it was his Christian duty (he was very devout) to
engage the whole power of France in an action designated to maintain
an impossible Latin kingdom in the Holy Land. All this may well have
influenced his decision. In any event, with the obstinacy of the vain, he
resolved to proceed with his crusade, if necessary alone.

Pope Eugenius III, anxious to avoid any apparent lack of zeal in the
defence of the faith, unenthusiastically issued a Bull authorising the
'taking of the Cross'; and Saint Bernard began his pious propaganda.
In doing so he provided one more instance of that frequent and always
surprising phenomenon, the man of talent carried away by his own
success. Defending with ardour, since this was his nature, a cause
which he had at first opposed, he convinced himself by the eloquence
of his own advocacy, and thereafter the Crusade became more Saint
Bernard's than the king's.

Bernard's preaching was one of the great pulpit triumphs of all time. At Vezelay, since there was not enough cloth for all those who wished to sew the cross to their cloaks, he tore his own clothes to pieces and distributed the fragments among his audience. In a style worthy of Abélard, he wrote to the Pope: 'I opened my mouth, I spoke, and immediately the crusaders were multiplied to infinity. The villages and towns are deserted. You would have difficulty in finding one man to every seven women. One sees nothing here but widows whose husbands are still alive.' It went so much to his head that he meddled in strategy, advocating the dispatch of the Emperor Conrad with a hundred thousand Germans against the pagan Slavs, and the King of Sicily's Normans against the infidels of Portugal and North Africa, while the French army made a dash for the Holy Places. But it was Suger who had to raise funds for the expedition.

The sovereign pontiff, come especially from Rome to bless the departure of the Crusade, arrived in Paris whilst Louis VII enjoyed days of glory, somewhat marred by a painful incident during the papal visit.

Eugenius III celebrated Mass at Saint-Geneviève, and the canons of the chapter of that church spread a splendid silk carpet before the altar. When the service was over the servants in the pope's suite folded the carpet and made to take it away, in accordance, with the ancient custom which gave them a right to any material on which the sovereign pontiff had knelt. The canons of Sainte-Geneviève did not see eye to eye with this. An altercation ensued between Roman deacons and Parisian priests, until after much wrangling and shouting the carpet was torn in halves. The parties then came to blows, grasping candelabra as weapons and sending for cudgels and reinforcements. Louis VII, attempting to intervene, was himself struck, and Pope Eugenius, seeing his servants with bloody faces and chasubles in shreds, roundly abused him, ordering him to do justice. The king, his face bruised, replied angrily: 'To whom shall I appeal, Most Holy Father, and who will do me justice, for when I intervened I too suffered from the anger of these furious men. You have the power to bind and unbind; very well then, hit them yourself!'

We may gather from this that the reform of the chapters, which Suger was so anxious to bring about, was perhaps a more urgent task than an expedition against the infidel, especially one beginning under such hopeful auspices.

6

Saint Bernard had been a little hasty in congratulating himself on having emptied towns and villages. The enthusiasm soon died down, and Louis VII led his army away amid the imprecations of the populace.

A Council of Government was appointed, but in fact it was Abbé Suger who, during the two years of the sovereign's absence, exercised the regency virtually single-handed, seeing to the administration of the functioning of its institutions, despite the grave news which continually reached the capital.

It was clear, even before the Crusade reached the Holy Land, that it would end in disaster. Month by month and week by week Paris was informed by couriers of the progress of the luckless venture. They heard that the Byzantines, Christian though they were, had refused to supply the crusaders with food, no doubt fearing a plan to seize Constantinople; that after a dispute between the French and Germans the Emperor Conrad had broken away from King Louis and been separately defeated by the Muslims; that the bulk of the French army had been annihilated in a defile in Anatolia, where soldiers, pilgrims, merchants, horses and baggage wagons had ended at the bottom of a precipice; and finally that the king, with what remained of his troops, had come by sea to the Latin settlement of Antioch where, to complete this succession of reverses, he had forfeited his honour as a husband.

For Louis VII had had the notion of taking his Princess of Aquitaine, brought up in the Languedoc Courts of Love, upon the crusade. It could have been a pleasanter journey. The stages were exhausting and under the interminable and cruel sun; there was constant danger of capture by the enemy and great shortage of food. Only a heroine or a woman deeply in love could have borne it. Eleanor came to detest the husband, more jealous than loving, who had compelled her to share this wretched adventure. At Antioch she fell into the arms of one of her youthful uncles, Raymond of Aquitaine, and, refusing to follow the king farther, demanded a separation on the grounds of their consanguineity.

Louis VII, inept as usual, called his lords to witness his misfortune and left Antioch under the eyes of the army, taking his wife with him by force.

Antioch is a long way from Paris, but rumours of the scandal soon filled the capital, accompanied by news of another military defeat even more disgraceful than those preceding it. Louis VII and Conrad, after patching up their quarrel at Damascus, had had the remnant of their forces cut to pieces. Moreover every messenger with bad news was also the bearer of further demands for money.

The real triumph of the crusade was that of Suger, who contrived, without imposing exceptional taxes or provoking riots, to meet the king's requirements, cover the loans he had extorted from his vassals, pay the ransom of prisoners and reimburse the considerable sums advanced by the Knights Templars. Indeed, a great many financial operations, transfers, credits, compensations, were carried out through the Order of the Temple, which became more or less the banking house of the Crusade, but which, although it had received its rule from Saint Bernard, none the less demanded the repayment of its advances.

Suger dealt with everything, debts and exceptional expenditure as well as the normal costs of internal administration, even maintaining the gratuities ordinarily distributed by the king. He succeeded by mulcting the treasury of Saint-Denis and also by sacrificing his own considerable fortune.

But public opinion was beginning to stir and become menacing. Saint Bernard himself suffered a serious eclipse of prestige and, overwhelmed by the disaster, began to doubt Providence, and even himself: 'The spirit of division is abroad among the princes,' he cried, 'and the Lord has led them astray into impracticable paths... We announced peace, and there is no peace; we promised success, and here is desolation. Assuredly God's judgements are just, but this one is a great abyss and I declare anyone happy who is not scandalised by it! I confess to being dishonoured by it.' Terrible words for a saint to utter.

The spirit of division was so infectious that the Count of Dreux, the king's brother, quarrelled with him, left Syria and returned to France, where he promptly turned the popular discontent to his advantage. A great movement in his favour spread among the nobles and was even felt in the Church. There was open talk of substituting him for the legitimate king, but Suger was on the watch, and wisely judged that France was in no condition to sustain a dynastic crisis. He hastily summoned an Assembly in Paris. The frail old man, alone against them all, threatened to have those who had organised the plot excommunicated by the Pope, and compelled the rebellious Count of Dreux publicly to disavow his enterprise. He did not, however, mince his words in the letters he wrote to the king. Pressing him to come home, he wrote: 'The disturbers of the kingdom have returned, and you, who should be here to defend it, remain like a prisoner in exile... You have handed

6*

over the lamb to the wolf, and the State to its ravishers... As for the queen, your wife, we counsel you, if you will, to conceal your resentment until, having come home by God's grace, you can settle that matter with all others.'

Louis VII finally decided to return to France, and he brought with him Eleanor, pregnant with a child which was not his. To this foolish monarch, the architect of his own misfortunes, Suger, like a good steward, handed over the kingdom intact with these words: 'Your judicial revenues, your taxes, your feudal dues, and the produce in kind of your domain have been preserved for you against your return. We have seen to it that your houses and palaces are in good order; those that were falling into ruin have been repaired. Your lands and your subjects, thanks be to God, enjoy peace.'

Acclaimed 'father of the nation' by the people of France, Suger died two years later, his political work a noble achievement.

His work in stone remains before our eyes in the form of the Church of Saint-Denis, which he rebuilt with remarkable rapidity immediately before the Crusade, when it seemed to him urgent and necessary to enlarge the royal church. It became, indeed, one of the most important places of pilgrimage not only in France but in all Europe, its attraction a mingling of history with piety.

Suger himself records crowds so dense on feast days that those who had visited the shrines and sought to leave struggled helplessly against the crush of those seeking to enter. Accidents were not infrequent. Women were 'squeezed as if in a press' and cried so loudly 'that one might have thought they were in childbirth'. People were sometimes trampled underfoot, and others were obliged to climb on to the heads of the men 'and walk over them as on a floor'. On more than one occasion the monks showing the reliquaries had to escape through the windows to save the holy bones.

The building of Saint-Denis had been conceived in the year that saw the completion of Vézelay. Suger so hastened the work that, twelve years later, the new abbey church could be consecrated. It became clear, even then, that although the building had been built as planned, it was too small. The people of Paris attended the consecration in such numbers that many more remained outside than were able to enter, and when the prelates emerged in procession to sprinkle the walls with holy water the crowd pressed in on them so dangerously that Louis VII, who was evidently fated to find himself in difficult situations in holy places, was obliged, with his officers, to strike at the people with sticks.

Suger had spared neither effort nor expense in building his new church. He had wanted splendid and inventive architecture and a richness of decoration in complete contrast to the barrenness of earlier churches. In this he was opposed to the mystical Saint Bernard, who preferred churches to be austere and was shocked by an excessive use of silver in religious ornaments. Suger believed that nothing could be too magnificent for the exultation of the divine majesty. Himself an administrator of worldly goods, he needed a display of outward show to express his religion.

It was at Saint-Denis that the Gothic form, which was to dominate ecclesiastical art and architecture for several centuries, first appeared. Whether we approve or not, whether we prefer the Romanesque for its dignity, purity and perfection, the fact remains that the cathedrals of Chartres, Amiens, Rheims, Notre-Dame de Paris and many others, those petrified forests of the faith, branchy, foliaceous, denticulated and diffusing through their windows the seven colours of God's gaze, are all in some degree Abbé Suger's grandchildren. And first among them is Notre-Dame.

2 MAURICE DE SULLY'S CATHEDRAL

The last advice Suger gave Louis VII was that he should not separate from Eleanor, but should put the interests of his kingdom above his grievances as a husband. But it was not advice that Louis VII had any intention of taking, and he obtained an annulment of his marriage from the Pope.

The consequence can be told in a thousand pages or in four words: it was the first Hundred Years' War.

Eleanor having taken her heart and her patrimony to Henry Plantagenet, Duke of Normandy and Count of Anjou, he promptly laid claim to Aquitaine, and war broke out between the two husbands. The cuckold was beaten. Of the two, one entirely succeeded and the other entirely failed. While Louis was summoning councils, Henry was mustering armies; while Louis lost Aquitaine, Henry became king of England; and while Louis was on pilgrimage to Compostella, Henry installed himself at Gisors.

Louis VII had no son by his second marriage, while Henry had four by Eleanor.

Less than ten years after Suger's death Louis had lost Brittany and Toulouse. A single great vassal, more powerful than his sovereign, on whom he imposed war or alliance as suited him best, held two-thirds of the kingdom; and the frontiers of the kings' power, continually contracting, had moved from the Pyrenees to Épernon and Montfort-l'Amaury, as in the time of Philip I.

Paris, the capital of this weakling king, must have been deeply attached to the Capet family for so dismal a reign to last another twenty years, making forty-three in all.

It was an unhappy reign but still not a negligible one, not by virtue of the king, but because of the kingdom, the people and the time. During that half-century a transformation took place in conscience, thought and education, in government and in the arts, which now we can clearly recognise. One has a sense of emerging from darkness; a purely subjective impression which simply means that we are beginning to encounter characteristics, in men and in society, that have endured to the present day.

Before this it is almost impossible for us to visualise Paris and the people living in it; a great effort of the imagination is required. But from the middle of the twelfth century human behaviour follows a more familiar pattern in which we may discern, if not an exact identity, at least a direct link with ourselves. The people of the twelfth century no longer seem to be abstractions; their problems become familiar, their language comprehensible. We can share their states of mind, their anxieties, their difficulties and their reasons for anger. We are better supplied with information and anecdotes about them, not only because the chroniclers increase in number, or because the records of public life are better preserved, but above all because these records are more immediately readable to us, and their anecdotes more directly expressive. In plain terms, from the twelfth century onwards people come to resemble us; we can only write the history of their ancestors, but about them we can write a novel. In defining great concepts they tended to use words in the way we do today. The fact that Suger was called 'the father of the nation' is significant; the term *patrie* existed in the language, but it had not yet appeared as designating France. And the debate between Abélard and Saint Bernard still concerns us.

There is something else which brings us closer to the people who lived under Louis the Young: it is the buildings, raised at that period, which we still use. So long as one uses an object—a tool, a windmill, a bridge or a church—for its original purpose, one remains linked to the men who made it. When, to witness a play or a bull-fight, we sit in the tiers of the theatre at Orange or the arena at Arles, we are descendants of Augustus or Marcus Aurelius. The inhabitants of Paris who today enter Notre-Dame to hear the Lenten sermon or attend a Te Deum are still contemporaries of Louis the Young.

The ancient episcopal church, built in the sixth century, had, like Saint-Denis, become too small; moreover, in spite of the fact that its chapter was exceedingly rich, it was on the point of falling into ruin. It was Bishop Maurice de Sully who rebuilt it.

This Sully had no family or feudal link with the Sully of Henri IV. He was a peasant's son, born in the village of Sully-sur-Loire. A good theologian and a remarkable orator, he had been Abélard's pupil; and he belonged more to the tradition of Suger than to that of Saint Bernard. He was made Bishop of Paris in 1160; and three years later the rebuilding of Notre-Dame began.

A street, the Rue Neuve-Notre-Dame, was cut to make it easier to bring the masonry. Pope Alexander III, being in Paris, blessed the laying of the foundation stone. Thomas à Becket, who had quarrelled with Henry Plantagenet and was a guest of the King of France, watched the walls of Notre-Dame rise from the ground, before returning to England to be murdered in his own Cathedral of Canterbury.

The altar was consecrated by a papal legate, the Cardinal of Albano, nineteen years after the work had begun. Shortly afterwards the Patriarch of Jerusalem, Heraclius, preached the Third Crusade in Notre-Dame in a nave that was still open to the sky, and to which there was access from the square by a flight of thirteen steps. For one did not enter it, as one does today, at ground level. The crust of time, the alluvial deposit of generations, has raised the level to the height of those thirteen steps.

When Maurice de Sully died, after thirty-six years as bishop, the great doorway and the two towers had still to be built, and it is not even certain that the roof had been completed. So the creator of Notre-Dame never saw the façade of his building, a façade which has since become the symbolic image of Paris throughout the world, standing for it as the Parthenon does for Athens, the Colosseum for Rome, Westminster Abbey for London, and the Kremlin for Moscow. Two hundred years were to pass before the cathedral was finished, and Victor Hugo said of it: 'Great buildings, like great mountains, are the work of centuries.'

Paris must indeed have been rich in goods and labour to be able to undertake a work of such magnitude despite internal wars and ruinous expeditions overseas.

In 1165, in the chapel of the Palace, Bishop Maurice baptised a boy called Philippe Dieudonné Auguste. He was Louis VII's sole male heir, by a third marriage, and it was he who was to complete the face of Paris.

3 PHILIPPE AUGUSTE'S WILL

He had been christened Auguste because he was born in the month of August, under the sign of the Lion.

Child prodigies are generally to be found in the arts or letters, rarely in government; but by the time Philippe Auguste was fourteen, his father, Louis VII, had become prematurely senile and the son took up the seal of France, an act tantamount to declaring the dethronement of his father. At his order, all the castles which had formed part of his mother's dowry were seized. Against the wishes of his family and the great feudal lords he married the niece of the Count of Flanders, and thus added Artois, her marriage portion, to his realm. Since the Archbishop of Rheims opposed her coronation, he had the new queen crowned in Paris. He also imprisoned all the Jews in Paris, not as a religious persecution but as a fiscal measure—a rough but effective method of nationalising the banks—for he freed them on payment of the fifteen thousand marks needed to make up the Treasury deficit.

The following month the King of England landed in Normandy and ordered a general muster of his troops. Philippe replied in kind and announced that he would occupy Auvergne. The two sovereigns met at Gisors. We do not know exactly what passed between Henry Plantagenet, then nearly fifty, who owned half France, and the young Capet who controlled barely a quarter of it. We do not know what seduction that assured voice emerging from a childish mouth exercised upon the omnipotent duke-king. It was enough to persuade Henry to give up the war and acknowledge his duties as vassal towards his future lord. Philippe Auguste returned from Gisors having made an alliance with the Plantagenet which, for a time at least, was to give him a free hand.

Philippe Auguste was just fifteen when his father died. At twenty he had defeated a hostile coalition of Flanders, Hainault, Burgundy, Rheims and Champagne, Blois, Chartres, Sancerre, Nevers, Namur and Louvain. He had attacked north and south, and defeated the Count of Sancerre at Châtillon-sur-Loire; he had taken Senlis and checked the Count of Flanders outside Crépy-en-Valois. He had seized Saint-Quentin. He had concentrated two thousand knights and fourteen thousand men-at-arms against Philip of Alsace at Compiègne. He was so successful in purchasing defections and bribing traitors that the members of the coalition eventually attacked each other. He had used the Plantagenet as mediator, secured the neutrality of the Emperor of Germany, and demanded and obtained the Vermandois inheritance, the town of Amiens and sixty-five castles. He was twenty-one when he defeated the surviving member of the coalition, the Count of Burgundy, and brought him under his control.

During the next twenty years Philippe Auguste was to fight against England, first supporting Richard Coeur de Lion in his rebellion against his father Henry, and then the pretensions of John against his brother Richard. Finally he championed the rights of Arthur of Brittany, John's nephew, against John. Every English prince was his ally while in rebellion, but an enemy if he became king. His sworn word was never a hindrance to him, and he never lacked good reasons for breaking it. He took Maine, Brittany, Touraine and Anjou from England, as much by hard diplomatic work as by constant acts of war.

Turning every chance to his advantage, Philippe pounced on Tours, besieged Angers, marched into Saintonge, and received the keys of the city of Nantes. He entered Rennes, where no Capet had been since the beginning of the dynasty, and finally took Normandy itself, the cradle of the English royal family and the origin of its power. This he achieved by capturing, eight years after it had been built by Richard Coeur de Lion, the enormous Château-Gaillard at Andelys, the fortified gateway to the duchy, which had seemed destined to defy the crown of France for centuries.

Philippe Auguste suffered only two defeats, the first on his attempt to land in England, when his fleet was surprised and destroyed before even putting to sea. The second was his attempt to place his son on the

English throne. Though supported for a time by a faction of the English nobility, the future Louis VIII was forced to leave England, being hated by the people and unanimously rejected by the bishops. The two countries had become truly independent nations, neither of which would accept domination by the other.

During those twenty years Philippe Auguste also found time to go on a crusade—not with enthusiasm, but because he had to appease religious and popular opinion. He insisted that his rival, Richard Coeur de Lion, should go with him. But he remained only long enough to win a victory at Saint John of Acre, which impressed the Christian world if not the Moslems. Then declaring himself ill, he hurriedly returned to France, where he had matters of inheritance to arrange, leaving the Crusaders to quarrel among themselves and Richard Coeur de Lion to finish the Crusade a prisoner of the Emperor of Germany because he had thrown the Duke of Austria's standard in the mud. Philippe Auguste offered the Emperor fifteen thousand marks a month for as long as he held Richard captive.

During those same twenty years he resisted the papal demand that he should live with his second wife, Ingeborg of Denmark, to whom he had taken an irremediable aversion on their wedding night. Ignoring the Pope he took Agnes de Meranie as his third wife and the Holy See sought in vain to place his kingdom under an interdict. The majority of the bishops of France opposed the publication of the sentence. Philippe Auguste himself dismissed a papal legate in the following terms: 'We order you, in respect of this matter, and if you have nothing else to discuss, to remain in this country no longer.' In the language of today this would be called 'breaking off diplomatic relations'. The papacy eventually accepted the position and legitimised the children of the third marriage.

On his forty-ninth birthday Philippe Auguste won the battle of Bouvines against the Emperor Otto IV and an Anglo-German-Flemish coalition. This was the Valmy of the Middle Ages, for it was not only a victory of the king and his knights, but of the king and the common people, the first truly *national* battle.

With Suger, France had really become a country; with Philippe Auguste it was conscious of being a nation. Although during the second Hundred Years' War English armies returned and held nearly the whole country, their presence was resented as an occupation. Those of the ruling classes who espoused or served the English cause were no

more than 'collaborators', and during a century of vicissitudes France
was to have no rest until she had regained the identity of which
Philippe Auguste had first made her.

Subordination of all private interests to the central power, independence from the Holy See and the German Empire, the rejection
of interference by any foreign power in the affairs of the state, and an
even greater rejection of domination by a foreign power over any part
of the national territory—these political aims which Philippe pursued
and achieved throughout his reign were to be those of all the great kings
and ministers who followed him. They were the aims of Philip the
Fair and Marigny in destroying the order of the Templars and forcing
the papacy to take up residence in Avignon; of Charles V in regaining
the kingdom after the disasters of Crécy and Poitiers; of Louis XI,
Henri IV, Richelieu, and Louis XIV.

After Bouvines, Philippe Auguste still had ten years in which to
cement his achievement.

We have drawn in outline the life of this great king, probably the
most important of all French sovereigns, because it is inseparable from
Paris, where he was born, where he reigned, and which he transformed
as he did the whole kingdom. The 'testament' which he drew up before
leaving for the crusade, a long series of instructions for the conduct of
government during his absence, is an administrative masterpiece; no
power in the state could take advantage of the sovereign's absence,
or even of his death, to acquire mastery over the others.

These with a traditional claim to the appointment were made
regents—that is to say, the Queen Mother and the Archbishop of
Rheims. But they had no real authority. Philippe Auguste entrusted
the Treasury to the Knights Templar, but did not give them the key,
which he deposited with an official of the crown and six notables of
Paris, who also received the guardianship of the royal seal. On that
day the Paris bourgeoisie made its first appearance on the stage of
History.

In the same testament Philippe Auguste ordered that a report on the
state of the kingdom and the conduct of the royal functionaries should
be sent him every four months. Except in the case of murder, rape or
treason, none of the provosts or bailiffs—from whom the rank of
prefect and sub-prefect descends—could be dismissed or even transferred
without his consent. Finally, he forbade, even in the event of his death,
the levying of any extraordinary tax before his son achieved his

majority. Never since her beginning had France known such an administrator.

Philippe Auguste also decided, when he set off on crusade, 'to surround that part of Paris situated to the north of the Seine with a continuous wall well furnished with towers and fortified gates'. Thus the capital, the seat and centre of power, would be protected against attack. Subsequently, during the Bouvines coalition, he completed work by building another wall enclosing the south of the city. The original Gallo-Roman wall, rebuilt by Eudes and completed by Louis the Fat, enclosed only the twenty-five acres of the Cité, whereas Philippe Auguste's wall enclosed six hundred and twenty-five acres. Twenty feet high, and ten thick, it was flanked by thirty-three towers to the north of the Seine and thirty-four to the south. Twenty-four fortified gates provided entrance to the city. Upstream, an outpost called La Tournelle was built, while downstream two imposing towers were raised, facing each other, which history was to make famous. The first, which originally bore the name of La Tour Philippe Auguste, then of La Tour Philippe Hamelin, became the famous Tour de Nesles, the scene of a royal adultery which became a subject of legend. On the site of this tower the Institut was built, and the Académie Française sits more or less where Marguerite of Burgundy's bed once stood. The Tour du Louvre, the second tower, was the origin of that palace, so often enlarged, in which the Valois dynasty lived out its pomps and dramas.

Defended by its wall, Paris could begin to build in safety for the centuries to come. Its achievements during the reign of Philippe Auguste are astonishing. Not only was the work continued on Notre-Dame, but Sainte-Geneviève was rebuilt; and the districts of Saint-Honoré, Saint-Pierre, which became Saints-Pères, and les Mathurins — all named after the churches or monasteries founded in them — date from this time. Three royal hospitals were newly built, and three new aqueducts, the first since the Roman period; while numerous fountains, among them that of the Innocents, distributed pure water in quantity to replace the partially polluted water of the Seine. The Halles were built, more or less where they stand today, to provide greater hygiene for food and help to control prices. Among other developments of importance to the capital was the Parloir aux Bourgeois, in effect the first Hôtel de Ville, the seat of Parisian assemblies and of the municipal administration. Anyone in search of a detail perpetuating the memory of Philippe Auguste may find one to this day at every cross-roads in Paris. When he feared assassination by the agents of Coeur de Lion, Philippe formed the habit of going about escorted by guards armed with truncheons. The truncheons now carried by the police are descended directly from there.

It was also Philippe Auguste's personal decision which inaugurated the paving of streets. On a day in 1185, when he was twenty, the king, standing at a palace window, was offended by the stench rising from the wagons churning through the mud. The streets of Paris at that time were open sewers, as one can see from the scabrous (and untranslatable) names they were given: Merderais, Merderiaux, Merderelle, Tranpunais, Tirepet, Pet-au-Diàble, Fosse-au-Chieurs and many more. Indeed the names of the streets give one a better idea of what went on in them than many a longer description – the Rue Vide-Gousset, for instance, and Coupe-Gorge; and the Rue Val-d'Amour, which housed the same ancient profession as the Rue Pute-y-muce (whore-in-hiding) which has become the Rue du Petit-Musc.

Philippe Auguste, on that morning in 1185, sent at once for the Provost and ordered him to improve *la croisée de Paris*, that is to say, the two main streets crossing the city from east to west and from north to south. The Rues Saint-Martin and Saint-Jacques, Saint-Antoine and Saint-Honoré, were thus the first cobbled or rather flagged streets, for huge sandstone blocks about three feet square were used, from which we derive the expressions *être sur le carreau* and *rester sur le carreau*, which preceded *être sur le pavé* (to be down and out).

In every field Philippe's reign displayed his urge for organisation, sound finance and hygiene. In 1212 a Council was held in Paris which forbade priests to undertake more masses than they were able to celebrate, to share the profits of the same mass among themselves, or to allow a cleric of inferior rank to say the office in their place. It also forbade priests to farm out of their parishes, monks to wear white gloves or fur or other precious material, and nuns to dance, whether in their convents or elsewhere. The same Council advised prelates not to hear matins in bed and imposed on them the duty of visiting every church in their diocese from time to time. It forbade them to keep concubines, suppressed the feast of the sub-deacons of Notre-Dame on 26 December, which the people called the 'Feast of the Drunken Deacons', and put an end to the Feast of Fools on 1 January, when priests regaled themselves with blood-pudding and sausage in the churches, burned old shoes in the censers and marched in grotesque procession through the streets.

It would have been better, perhaps if the Council of 1212 had not ordered copies of Aristotle's *Metaphysics* to be burned in order to purify education. For with growing success of Abélard's school, the students had become a civic problem. They could find neither lodgings nor food at prices they could afford. To have their grievances heard, they formed themselves into large bands, came down from the mountain of Sainte-Geneviève, went in procession shouting through the streets, battled with the civic guards and even besieged the royal palace. The removal of a master, a difference of opinion between teachers and pupils or teachers and authority, was all that was needed to provoke these demonstrations. To prevent them the authorities rebuilt the Petit Châtelet, near Saint-Michel, which barred the students access to the Cité.

In 1200 Philippe Auguste proceeded to codify the studies of medicine, civil and canon law. He defined the privileges of masters and students. A committee consisting of two teaching masters and two citizens was set up to fix rents. Finally, in 1215, the designation *Universitas magistrorum et scholariorum*, appeared for the first time in an official act. The University of Paris had received its name. It was recognised as one of the great institutions contributing to public weal. In a sense, this act of 1215 was the Bouvines of the mind.

One can argue for ever about the influence of individual acts on the course of history. Certainly one sovereign is not enough to change a people, nor can a society be transformed unless the general conditions make it possible or neccessary. But at the right time there must appear one of those men we call 'great', who have the character, actions and are in power long enough to help a nation to become what it seeks to be. Great men do not make history; but it needs them, and history cannot be made without them. Or if it is, it is badly made.

The twelfth and thirteenth centuries witnessed the extraordinary accomplishments of two extraordinary men at opposite ends of the globe. Genghis Khan, that other prodigy, began at fifteen to create the Mongol power out of almost nothing, and he proclaimed himself Emperor of the Universe in the year that Philippe Auguste, having defeated the English, could feel that he was really King of France. Genghis Khan was born two years later than Philippe Auguste, and he died in 1227, four years after him. Their destinies run almost parallel, within the respective dimensions of Asia and France.

4 THE ARCHIVES OF SAINT LOUIS

Louis VIII passed too quickly to leave any enduring memory. His reign lasted three years and he died in suspicious circumstances. Weak in character and intelligence, he was distinguished only by his blunders in his attempt on the crown of England, and his brutality during the expedition against the Albigensians. His death was probably to the advantage of the kingdom.

As Philippe Auguste had once predicted, the government of France now fell into the hands of a woman and a young child. Blanche of Castille, granddaughter of the famous Eleanor, showed herself to be a woman of authority well able to maintain the prestige of royal power and see that its institutions worked. This remarkable queen taught France that a woman can have a head for politics; and, indeed, she was the first great queen worthy of note since Brunhilda. As Anne of Austria was later to rule with Mazarin, and perhaps with the same feelings towards him, Blanche had an Italian at her side, Frangipani, Cardinal-Deacon of San Angelo, who helped her to govern and to suppress a first *Fronde*, or uprising, of the great lords.

The Cardinal of San Angelo, a peremptory aristocrat, more knight than churchman, disliked the University of Paris, which returned the compliment. He had broken the University's seal, that is to say suppressed its privileges, and the University had sacked his house. The police pursued students among the vines, killing some and throwing others in the river. Things became so bitter that masters and pupils dispersed to Rheims, Angers, Orleans and Toulouse, or were taken in by the rival schools of England, Italy and Spain. In 1231, the Pope had to intervene to reconstitute the University.

Blanche of Castille remained joint ruler even when her son had attained his majority.

Louis IX has always been the model King of France. For seven centuries mothers have held him up as an example, the king who was so careful to say his prayers, the good son who, even when he came of age and became glorious and all powerful, invited his mother to preside over his councils and made her sit beside him to receive ambassadors. Schoolmasters have praised the virtues of this modest prince who so loved justice that he delighted in rendering it to the poor, under the oak of Vincennes. But the man cannot be reduced to such simple terms. The strangeness of his character and his psychological complexities

made him extraordinary, more so indeed in his person than in his
acts of government. He was one of the great neurotics of history. Had
he not inclined to saintliness he might have been a monster. Neros are
made of the same fibre. We have much detailed evidence about him, all
tending to show that, in his most startling effect on people, he would
have made an admirable subject for psycho-analysis.

The son of a dominant mother who terrified him with threats of the
Devil, and by telling him from his earliest childhood that she would
rather see him dead than guilty of mortal sin, he was haunted all his
life by the fear of sin and death, and developed a morbid anxiety
that he might die unshriven. Hence his excessive devotions, his fifty
genuflexions and as many Ave Marias before retiring to bed, the
two masses he heard on rising, one low one for the dead, which
were followed throughout the day by the offices of tierce, sext,
nones, vespers and compline. All this can scarcely have helped him in
the performance of his administrative duties. Even on horseback,
when travelling or at war, he would halt his retinue at the hour of
the office and order his chaplains to chant as they sat on their horses
around him.

He mortified himself by wearing a hair-shirt, although his confessor
repeatedly told him that the practice was unsuited to his royal state, and
he bestowed similar shirts on his family and friends as the most
precious gift he could make them.

He imposed privations of every kind upon himself and was wretched
if he happened to laugh on a Friday. His besetting need for absolution
and expiation drove him not only to increase his penances and alms-
giving, but to bring the most repellant beggars into the Palace of the
Cité, so that he might eat with them and even serve them with his own
hands. He even alarmed the Church with his passion for self-humilia-
tion; and father abbots, such as that of Royaumont, had great difficulty
in preventing him from summoning all the abbey's monks so that he
might wash their feet.

Public opinion had little liking for this exaggerated piety, which
seemed unworthy of a king. Louis IX was laughed at and people
called him 'Brother Louis'. He was even insulted on occasion, for men
shouted at him that he was the king of priests rather than of France.
These moments may well have afforded him some gratification, with
their foretaste of martyrdom.

So that he might go on washing their feet without risk of disgracing his royal majesty he had blind beggars collected and secretly brought to him at the Palace.

When he spent the night with his wife, he always rose at midnight to go to matins, though he did not dare to kiss the reliquaries. When he was dying he refused to take chicken broth because it was a fast day and his confessor had not given him a dispensation.

But he had other aspects besides those that look absurd to us, as they did to his contemporaries. When famine raged in any part of the kingdom Louis IX did not rest until supplies of food had been dispatched. To his charity, which was real and deep, Paris owed the foundation of the Filles-Dieu, a home for prostitutes, the Hospice of the Quinze-Vingts, which sheltered three hundred blind people, and the house in the Rue Coupe-Gueule for 'sixteen poor masters of arts' preparing their doctorates of theology. These students were lodged free and learned clerks were appointed to direct their studies. The chaplain was Robert de Sorbon, and the house has become the Sorbonne. Other institutions were founded on the model of this first 'college' to receive the students of many 'nations'—from Scotland, Sweden, Germany or Constantinople. It was the first 'Cité universitaire', and it contained fifteen thousand students.

To Saint Louis's piety Paris owes the Sainte-Chapelle,—that masterpiece of Gothic architecture, which was built in two years. Its daring spire, springing in stone towards the sky, is like the mast that was lacking to the eternal ship.

Louis IX was immensely tall, slender and fine-drawn, his figure bowed by fasting and mortification. He dressed in the commonest stuffs and furs, but wore peacock's feathers in his hat.

His austerity was oppressive. He never addressed anyone with the familiar *tu*, and this undoubtedly contributed to the increased use of the formal *vous* in France. He would not tolerate loose talk, bawdy songs or games, and in fact did not like people to enjoy themselves. He was harsh with the people about him and his outbursts were often cruel, but at the same time he disliked hurting people and would try to console the person he had wounded. Being unpredictable in his reactions and inaccessible to ordinary human sentiments, he was surrounded by passionate devotion.

For although he loved France as though identifying it with the image of his mother, and God as a fatherless child may love Him, he did not love men. He took note of their diversity but did not understand their differences. If he washed their feet, it was to make himself like the Saviour; but in his royal role he modelled himself on God the Father, the supreme magistrate, judging the faults and merits of each man in accordance with a single absolute law. And absolute law, in matters of faith, was dogma, the framework on which Saint Louis relied.

His religion was inflexible. Seeking goodness and striving greatly for it in himself, he took no account of human suffering, or of human life if dogma were disputed and his certainties imperilled. It was he who officially installed the Inquisition in France.

At the same time he could be surprisingly naïve. He paid all the debts of the Latin Emperor of Constantinople, accepting in exchange nothing but the Holy Crown of Thorns, intact, which was the more surprising since there was already a piece of the same relic in France. He had more than one characteristic in common with his ancestor Robert the Pious.

While Louis IX did his utmost to prevent war in his own lands, where he hated the spilling of blood, he was delighted to join a crusade, and was proud of slaughtering the infidel. It seemed to have a liberating effect on him. He no longer feared death, bore his armour nobly, conducted himself with admirable courage, and even laughed. The skirts of Blanche of Castille did not extend beyond French territory.

Louis IX was irrational and given to wild fancies. He dreamed of converting Islam. He believed the Emperor Michael Palaeologus, who promised to make him arbiter in a proposal of union (already!) between the Roman and Eastern churches, if he would not pass through Constantinople.

He set out on his final expedition from Aigues-Mortes one First of July, helmeted in high summer, intending to sail through the Mediterranean and deliver Jerusalem. He took his three sons with him, despite the Pope's advice and the obvious dangers to the succession; but he got no farther than Tunis, where the sun and an outbreak of plague in his army defeated him.

Religious problems may be summarily disposed of in the light of dogma, but civil affairs are more difficult. In his anxiety to give every man his due Louis IX sometimes delivered judgements of such complexity that they became a source of endless dispute both at home and abroad. In civil law, as in religion, he needed a framework, and he looked for it in the past, in custom and tradition. Profoundly conservative, he played into the hands of the feudal lords, who quickly claimed, as if they were legal rights, the privileges they had acquired

before Philippe Auguste. For the next two centuries the landowners of France clamoured incessantly for a return to 'the good customs of Saint Louis', and quoted them in support of their demands. Louis IX's word as a legislator, which for a long time was to be considerable, consisted mainly in consolidating the privileges of the strong.

His attitude had at least one positive result from which we still benefit. That he might know the rights of all men, and thus give enlightened justice, Louis IX caused to be collected in the Palace, catalogued and preserved, all royal acts, titles to property, treaties, customs of various fiefs, charters of towns and guilds, edicts and judgements. These were the first Archives.

Since then France has had a memory into which lawyers, historians and novelists can delve, and it is lodged in the capital as in a brain. The Sainte-Chapelle, the Sorbonne and the Archives are the three gifts Saint Louis bestowed on Paris. Nor is the third the least, for, continually enriched, it bears witness to the 'work of the centuries'.

French history after Saint Louis can no longer be written in the same way. We may almost say, without too great a paradox, that from then on Paris was to change no more. Her appearance and dimensions might change — indeed, how greatly! — but not her nature or her innate characteristics. All the organs of public life, like those of a living body, had come into existence, had found their place and, on the whole, were to retain it. The houses would be rebuilt again and again, just as cell tissue renews itself. The streets would grow wider, as the arteries develop during growth, and one day would begin to become afflicted with sclerosis.

Paris was to grow longer, but concentrically, like a tree. As we count the years in the section of a tree, so we can measure ring by ring on successive maps of Paris, the work of the centuries, history's cold winters and the rich summers of prosperity.

The bridges were to multiply, but in the image, reflected to either bank by the waters of the Seine, of the first bridge of all, which Caesar crossed.

DATE DUE

MAR 1 1			
GAYLORD			PRINTED IN U.S.A.